FROM IMPASSE
TO INTIMACY

FROM IMPASSE TO INTIMACY

HOW UNDERSTANDING UNCONSCIOUS NEEDS CAN TRANSFORM RELATIONSHIPS

DAVID SHADDOCK

JASON ARONSON INC.
Northvale, New Jersey
London

Production Editor: Robert D. Hack

This book was set in 11 pt. Veljovic by Alpha Graphics of Pittsfield, New Hampshire.

Library of Congress Cataloging-in-Publication Data

Shaddock, David.
    From impasse to intimacy: how understanding unconscious needs can transform relationships / by David Shaddock.
      p. cm.
    Includes bibliographical references and index.
    ISBN 0-7657-0163-4
    1. Marriage—United States.   2. Married people—United States—
Psychology.   3. Man–woman relationships—United States.
4. Intimacy (Psychology)   I. Title.
HQ734.S517   1998
306.81—DC21   98-10301

Printed in the United States of America on acid-free paper. For information and catalog write to Jason Aronson Inc., 230 Livingston Street, Northvale, New Jersey 07647. Or visit our website: http://www.aronson.com

∽ For Toby ∾

Contents

Acknowledgments

I want to begin by acknowledging my two psychotherapy mentors, Barbara Safran, L.C.S.W. in family therapy and Dr. Susan Sands in self psychology, for their invaluable role in shaping my professional development. My deepest gratitude also goes to Robert Jupe, L.C.S.W., for his years of teaching by example. My present collaboration with Dr. Jeff Trop and my sister, Dr. Luba Fischer, has contributed greatly to the ideas in this book. I would also like to thank the members of my psychotherapy discussion group, Whitney van Nouhuys, Bob Shaw, and Steve Galper, for years of intellectual challenge and support. My students at John F. Kennedy University have offered me invaluable feedback on the relevance of my ideas to their personal and professional lives.

Many people have made significant contributions over the life of this project. Peter Beren helped shape the project at its inception. Jeremy Tarcher and Andrea Stein made significant editorial contributions. Phyllis Hatfield provided invaluable help in editing Part I of the manuscript. My deepest gratitude goes to Cindy Hyden, who with humor, patience, and intelligence helped shape most every page of the book.

I want to thank the people who have read parts of the manuscript or who have offered physical help, including Susan Griffin, Esther Furash, Luba Fischer, Jo Robinson, Tamara Schoenaberg, Vernon Lawton, and, most importantly, Hope Hutman.

Finally I would like to express my deepest gratitude to my children, Jennifer and Jacob, for teaching me the absolute importance of connection, and to my wife, Toby, for her patience and support for this project and for her love, strength, and wisdom for twenty-five years.

A Journey
to Living
Unison

What man most passionately wants is his living wholeness, and his living unison, not his own isolate salvation
of his "soul."

D. H. Lawrence

I first saw the quote from D. H. Lawrence on a poster in my dentist's office. The poster was a line drawing of a couple dancing together—living unison. I realized that what Lawrence meant by "living wholeness" and "living unison" was our ability to be in relationship, and that what he meant by the "isolate salvation of his soul" was the exaggerated value we placed on our separateness.

The belief that our healing and salvation come not through isolation but through relationship inspired me to write this book. I began with two passions: to correct the misconceptions that lead people to feel that their marriages are failures, or that change is impossible; and to give people a way of looking at their relationships that would build compassion, forgiveness, and the possibility of growth. I wanted to write a book that would emphasize understanding ourselves and our partners, rather than just offer prescriptions. At the same time, I wanted to provide practical help for couples in applying this understanding to long-term patterns of conflict or emotional distance, as well as to everyday struggles about such issues as sex, money, housework, and in-laws.

The book is informed by my convictions that:

- Dependency is healthy and normal.
- Relationships are the best place to solve individual psychological problems.
- Childhood experiences unconsciously affect and often distort the way we see our partners.
- Everyday conflicts become power struggles because they come to symbolize childhood issues.
- We create and sustain dysfunctional patterns of relating to provide protection from even greater pain.
- Understanding the protection these stuck patterns and power struggles offer is a starting place for working on the relationship.
- Transformation is possible, even in the most hopeless and painful relationships, if the partners can come to feel empathy for each other.

- Decoding symbolic issues to uncover the invisible needs and fears is the best way to build that empathy.

For the last twenty years I have been trying to understand the way relationships work. My quest has led me to look at the way our society does and does not support our relationships. It has led me to study and try to integrate recent thinking in the fields of psychoanalysis, family systems theory, and child development research. It has led me to examine my own marriage and to try to replace stuck and painful patterns of relating with ones that provide greater intimacy.

MARRIAGE IN TODAY'S SOCIETY

We live in an age that values the individual. Our heroes are entrepreneurs and adventurers. The human potential movement of the last thirty years places tremendous emphasis on self-awareness and personal growth. Even the social movements of our time strive for new and important individual freedoms.

All this emphasis on individuality has brought benefits. We are a productive, self-reliant society with great opportunities for individual freedom and expression. But it has also brought serious liabilities. Half of all of our marriages end in divorce. Many of the most vulnerable members of the community suffer from neglect. And values of cooperation and connection often take a back seat to values of success and individual initiative. The very word *dependent* is negative in our society.

Often a couple in pain feel terribly isolated. They have no images in the media that accurately reflect the experiences they are having. They have unrealistically idealistic views of relationship and feel ashamed that they are not living up to those ideals. They don't know that everyday issues such as money, housework, and sex have tremendous symbolic power, and they feel petty and ashamed that these issues have aroused so much passion or seem so unsolvable. Their friends don't talk about what really goes on in their relationships, probably because of their own shame.

Faced with a society that puts more emphasis on independence than on healthy dependence, many couples come to see the choice as one of individual growth versus commitment to marriage and family. I was recently at a conference where one of the speakers urged the audience not to cling to relationships that they had outgrown because of their spiritual development. Confronted with these perceptions, and finding little validation for our dependency needs, we have framed our choice between unhappily staying in or guiltily leaving a relationship.

Many of the couples I work with are quite surprised when I congratulate them for the positive contributions they are making to each other's welfare. They are either in too much pain to see that any mutual caring still exists, or they are too used to looking at the negative to pay it any attention. Equally important, they are unaware that the pain in relationships offers an opportunity for necessary growth. "You are your husband's best hope of learning to overcome his fear of intimacy," I'll tell a wife. "Don't give up and start patronizing her," I'll tell a husband, "you are here to help her learn to stick up for herself."

We may think of our lives as individual journeys, with our own goals of career and accomplishments, but few of us think of relationship itself as a journey. We are so busy pursuing Lawrence's "isolate salvation of our soul" that we do not strive for the "living unison" of a vibrant, committed involvement with another human being. The journey into the living unison of relationship can be an authentic adventure. What is riskier than letting another human see the parts of ourselves we have always kept hidden behind a wall of shame? And what is more growth-enhancing than finding our partner's acceptance?

A NEW VIEW OF HUMAN NATURE

It is almost one hundred years since Freud introduced the revolutionary theory of the unconscious mind. Since that time, a great deal of research has gone into the study of our individual psyches. We have focused on understanding our dreams, our deepest motivations, and our inner conflicts. This effort has opened up great vistas of human understanding, and has made way for advances in the therapeutic treatment of individual problems. Until recently, however, psychoanalysis has been overly influenced by Freud's assumptions about human nature. These assumptions have prevented psychologists from developing an understanding of the central role relationships play in our lives.

Writing at the end of the Victorian era, which had seen the final triumph of colonialism and the introduction of Darwin's theory of the survival of the fittest, Freud emphasized individual instinctual drives as the basis for human behavior. It was a kind of "every man for himself" psychology, where humans were all seen as trying to fulfill deep-seated, instinctual needs.

Recent advances in the study of early childhood development have called some of Freud's theories into serious question. These scientists see *relationship* as the most important element in a child's development. They focus their attention not on the child's need to express certain instinctual drives, but on his need to be psychologically bonded to the caregiving parent. They find that our earliest and deepest human need is to be in a loving relationship that is attuned to our emotional needs. This need is the very basis of human existence.

At the same time these child development specialists are stressing the importance of relationship in child development, new schools of psychoanalysis are emphasizing that our individual psyches are continually influenced by relationships. The object relations school, while still retaining Freud's emphasis on instinctual drives, emphasizes the way early relationships shape development. The relational school of psychoanalysis is greatly influenced by the work of the late Heinz Kohut. Kohut trained in Vienna before coming to the United States to flee Nazi terror. He was a leading theorist in classical Freudian psychoanalysis, but grew dissatisfied with Freud's emphasis on drives and internal psychic structure. In place of Freud's model of the mind as made up of internal structures (id, ego, and superego) operating in conflict with each other, Kohut saw the *self* as the basic unit, a self that seeks wholeness and fragments only when the relationships that support it fail. Where Freud saw the psyche as determined by invariant structures that are developed in early childhood, Kohut's self was sustained at all times by the care of others. Kohut's self psychology was at the heart of a paradigm shift in psychoanalysis. Rather than see the analyst as curing the patient by helping him make his unconscious drives conscious, Kohut and his followers believed that it was the positive relationship with the analyst that was curative.

Another source of my understanding of relationships draws on my training as a family therapist. Family systems theory does not study people as individuals at all. It emphasizes our interconnectedness, the fact that we operate as part of an intricate network of relationships. Our individual behavior can only be understood in the context of these relationships. Family systems theory studies the patterns of relationships themselves, rather than the inner worlds of the individual partners.

Too often, however, family therapy has focused on changing behavior, to the exclusion of understanding the unconscious feelings and beliefs that shaped it. In the last ten years many theorists have worked to combine the new theories of psychoanalysis with systems theory. Foremost among them are Robert Stolorow and colleagues whose theory of intersubjectivity holds that human behavior can only be understood within the context of relationship systems. My own work grows out of this synthesis.

Combining a systems view of relationships with our new understanding of the central role relationships play in our individual psyches has allowed us, for the first time, to begin to understand the yearnings that bring us together and the fears and conflicts that keep us apart. What I call the *invisible marriage* embodies the unconscious and systemic factors that influence the way we feel and behave in intimate relationships.

If our salvation, as Lawrence suggests, is to come not from isolation but from connection, we must begin by accepting our own confusing and contradictory feelings toward our partners. The invisible marriage is not a type of pathology. It is a term that describes the way we love here, struggling with needs that can never be fully met and with fears that can overwhelm us, living our lives together, as Denise Levertov says in her poem "The Ache of Marriage," "Two by two in the ark of/the ache of it."

I

Origins of the Invisible Marriage

1

Why
Love Is
Blind

Love looks not with the eyes but with the mind
Therefore is winged Cupid painted blind

SHAKESPEARE

Every day in my practice as a marriage and family therapist I see people who want more love and intimacy in their lives:

- Wendy and Lee, a young professional couple with two children, have had the same fight for the last three years. Wendy claims that Lee just doesn't understand what it takes to manage a career and a household at the same time, while Lee feels that Wendy just "isn't on my side" when "it's crunch time" at his demanding job. Instead of supporting each other, their communication centers on putting each other down.
- Julie, a newly married nursing student, after only a year of marriage, complains that she is desperate for more contact with her husband, Matt, and says that she "can't stand his silent treatment anymore," while Matt, an electrician, seems genuinely puzzled about why the nice woman he married has become so "negative, angry, and critical."
- Bill and Evelyn, an attractive couple in their mid-fifties, arrived at a time in their lives to which they had long looked forward, when their kids were grown and they were finally free to "live for ourselves," only to find that they were like "two trains moving on parallel tracks," with less and less to talk about to each other.
- Judith and Daniel, a young couple, thought they'd arrived at the perfect solution for raising a family: Daniel would put his career on hold for the first three years and raise their son, Adam, while Judith got established in her medical practice. Despite their best laid plans this arrangement only led to bitter resentments between them, with Daniel angry at Judith for ignoring him and Adam, and Judith withdrawing even more after Daniel's angry outbursts.

All of these people have tried hard to improve their relationships. They have tried to change their behavior and they have tried to change their partners' behavior. They may have read one of the many books on relationships that urge them to fight more fairly, or communicate their feelings more clearly. But nothing has worked for them.

A crucial piece is missing from their understanding of their relationships. They do not completely know what their fight is about, or why they are having such strong feelings. They have been looking at the *visible* aspects of their relationships—the things they say and do. But all of these problems stem not from the visible, objective parts of the relationship but from the subjective world of the unconscious mind. Trying to make sense of them by looking at rational behavior is like trying to look at an elephant through a microscope: you're simply using the wrong lens.

In addition to the parts of ourselves that are immediately available to our awareness, such as the things we actually do and say, each of us contains vast areas of subjectivity, where our thoughts and feelings move more in symbols than in words. This is the realm of our unconscious minds. It is the realm of dreams, the realm of automatic emotional responses such as anger or fear, and the realm where our childhood memories of the pleasure and pain of our earliest relationships are stored.

A modern psychologist might rephrase Shakespeare's acute observation that opens this chapter, "Love looks not with the eyes but with the *unconscious* mind." In *A Midsummer Night's Dream* the fairy princess Titania swallows a potion that causes her to fall in love with a common worker, Bottom, who has been transformed into an ass. The potion is made of the hopes and romantic yearnings of her unconscious mind, which has distorted what her eyes are seeing into what it wants to see. This can also work in just the opposite way. Most of us have had the experience of feeling that our partner, who had once seemed so desirable, now seems like a complete ass. Here our unconscious fears are negatively distorting or exaggerating reality.

The unconscious dynamics of relationships can have painful, even tragic effects. Without an understanding of the unconscious dynamics of relationships, blame and guilt flourish. We see the hurtful things our partner does and think that he or she is being willfully and inexplicably cruel. We watch ourselves lash out in anger and feel that we must be defective to act that way. And we see the areas of struggle and pain in the relationship as evidence that we have made the wrong choice in a partner.

On the other hand, when we begin to be aware of the deeper reasons for our own and our partner's behavior, something very powerful happens. Blame and guilt are replaced by understanding and compassion. Issues that seemed insurmountable now lend themselves to compromise. Two enemies battling over scarce emotional resources can become two allies advocating for each other's growth and fulfillment. Problems in the relationship become challenges for personal growth.

THE UNCONSCIOUS MIND AND RELATIONSHIPS

In the Rorschach test, subjects are asked to make up a story about an ink blot. The test works to reveal the contents of our unconscious minds because we have a tendency to project our unconscious fears and fantasies into the picture.

Relationships work in a very similar fashion. Consider Matt and Julie, one of the couples introduced at the beginning of this chapter. Matt is a self-described introvert, who spends his days thinking about the problems that come up in his work as an electrician. In his words, he needs "a few moments to himself to chill out" when he gets home. When they first started seeing each other, Julie saw Matt's quiet nature as a sign of his inner strength, but lately Matt's silences, especially his lack of warmth when he comes home from work, have become intolerable to her. The trait that once meant "here's a man I can trust" now means "I am going to be painfully abandoned forever."

Julie's father, a rancher, died when she was 12 years old. She describes herself as "Daddy's girl." Both her positive and negative reactions to Matt were unconscious projections of that event onto her present-day situation. When she met Matt, her unconscious mind told her that she had finally found a replacement for her father. But when she began to feel abandoned by him, her unconscious mind told her that the worst trauma of her life was about to be repeated.

Julie's story illustrates two important points about the way the unconscious mind affects relationships. The first is that it projects childhood experiences onto the present. The unconscious mind will always mistake our partners for our parents. The technical term for this is *transference*. And the second is that the unconscious mind contains both our deepest yearnings and our deepest fears about relationships.

Julie's life was altered forever by her father's death. She stopped being "Daddy's girl" and immediately became a "little adult," taking care of her mother and her younger sister. So complete was this transformation that in adulthood she was completely unaware of her yearning to feel like the special child again. This yearning was directly connected to her deepest fear: if she lets herself feel special to someone, that person might suddenly disappear, just as her father had done. For Julie, as for most of us, her deepest yearnings and her deepest fears were knitted together into a tight ball of emotions. And the source of her emotions was largely invisible to her.

In relationship, each partner's unconscious fears and yearnings encounter the other's. Despite our conscious intentions, these unconscious fears and yearnings control our experience of the relationship. They are like the stagehands in a theater production. They set up the props and backdrops that form the background to our relationship, they play the background music that heightens our emotions, and at key times they hit a particular speech or action with a powerful spotlight that sets it apart from the rest of the action. While what we see is what happens "onstage" between ourselves and our partners, our unconscious fears and yearnings are busy controlling the meanings we attach to those actions. The term *invisible marriage* refers to the unconscious factors that control how we feel and act in relationships.

MATT AND JULIE'S INVISIBLE MARRIAGE

When Matt and Julie came to me for therapy, it was clear to both of them that their marriage was in trouble. I was struck by how quickly the situation had deteriorated. They had been married just over a year, during which time their relationship had changed from one that sparkled with affection to one in which the same angry accusations and sullen avoidance were repeated almost nightly. Neither Matt nor Julie had a clear idea of what had happened or why. They understood neither the unconscious yearnings that brought them together nor the unconscious fears that were now driving them apart. To understand more about their invisible marriage, we need to know also about Matt's childhood. Matt was the eldest of three brothers. He characterized his parents' marriage as "angry but cool." "The only time they really got together," Matt told me, "is when they were criticizing one of the kids." As the oldest, Matt came in for the lion's share of that criticism. As a way of protecting himself from it he drew inside himself. He had few friends in high school, preferring to take long bike rides or work alone on his several hobbies.

Matt's mother had once been a vivacious, intelligent woman. She was bitterly disappointed in her husband's career and in the lack of warmth in their relationship. Unconsciously, Matt yearned for his mother's approval and wished that he could be connected to her vitality. When he met Julie, he felt that his wish had come true. She was young and alive, and, most importantly, seemed to accept him uncritically. But now his deepest yearnings had been replaced by his deepest fears. Julie seemed the very incarnation of his parents: critical, unfair, arbitrary. Matt reacted to Julie just as he had to his parents—he withdrew inside himself. Of course, for Julie, Matt's withdrawal seemed to confirm that her worst abandonment fears were coming true. The couple's reactions were mutually reinforcing: the more Julie got angry the more Matt withdrew, and the more Matt withdrew the angrier Julie got.

Matt and Julie's relationship was at a critical juncture. They might react to their unhappiness by breaking up, but it was equally possible that they would settle into a disappointing but stable pattern in which Julie angrily yet doggedly pursued contact with Matt, while he just as stubbornly retreated behind his walls. Such a solution is not uncommon. Just this kind of stable, if unhappy pattern characterizes the pursuit/avoidance script discussed in Chapter 5.

THREE STAGES OF THE INVISIBLE MARRIAGE

Most relationships undergo three phases: a hopeful or *honeymoon* phase, a period of *struggle and disappointment*, and a period of *accommodation*. In the honeymoon phase, feelings are dominated by unconscious yearnings, such as Julie's yearning to recreate her relationship with her father. In this phase we believe that our partners will fulfill our deepest needs to be admired and understood.

But then something disappointing happens: a conflict develops, or traits we haven't seen before in our partner emerge. Now our feelings are dominated by our deepest fears, such as Julie's fear of being abandoned or Matt's fear of being unfairly criticized. This inaugurates a period of disappointment and struggle. We are plagued with doubts about our choice, and wonder if we should stay with the relationship.

Eventually, if we do stay together, the relationship settles into a fixed pattern. This fixation is the hallmark of the accommodation phase. Sometimes we simply get used to the conflict, which goes on more or less continuously. Other times we develop a strategy for avoiding each other, and live separate lives under the same roof. The need for protection from deep emotional pain predominates in the accommodation phase. Relationships become predictable, and painful surprises are avoided.

MAKING A DIFFERENT CHOICE

I wanted to provide Matt and Julie with a third choice, other than breaking up or settling for an unhappy marriage, but first I needed to know if they were committed to working on the relationship. "What this is going to take," I told them, "is coming to know yourself and your partner in a whole new way—a way that will involve coming to terms with some painful truths about each of you." Matt was eager. "I know I really love Julie, and I'd hate to lose her." Julie was more reluctant. "I just don't know if I want to spend the rest of my life with someone who won't even talk to me."

"I'm not asking you to commit to settling for the status quo," I answered. "What I am asking is that you commit to finding out why Matt has become so withdrawn, and why you get so angry when he does withdraw." When I put it this way, Julie agreed.

The next time I saw Matt and Julie, they were in a deep crisis. One night the week before, they had started to bicker. Julie had been telling Matt about starting her practicum at the local hospital. She looked over and found Matt fiddling with one of their appliances, apparently not listening at all. She blew up at him, and they exchanged heated words. As the fight escalated, Matt had said he needed to get away, to "clear his head." He did not come home until one in the morning.

I was not really surprised at this, and I told them so. "Each of you made a commitment to be more vulnerable to each other last week. That can be scary, and can leave you being more reactive to the things your partner does that cause you pain. Let's try and get underneath some of the anger and find out what was going on in this fight. After all, it started over something that seems on the surface to be pretty small. You, Julie, were trying to tell Matt something important that happened to you, and you thought he was listening, but then you looked up and found him fiddling with the toaster. What did you say then?"

Matt answered. "She said, 'Put that thing down. You already broke the VCR last week.'"

"And what did you do?"

"I just turned and walked into the living room."

By slowing down the action, I was able to help Matt and Julie see how this incident perfectly enacted their worst fears about relationships, fears that went back to their childhood. For Julie the issues were about surprises and abandonment. "It's as if I closed my eyes and you were there, and then I opened them and you had disappeared."

"Just like your father disappeared?" I asked.

"I used to tell myself that he had just gone away, that he'd come back any day," she replied, her eyes starting to tear up. "Sometimes I'd get to believe that, and I'd feel happy for an hour, or even a day. And then I'd come back to reality and feel silly."

The traumatic pattern of her childhood had been replayed in the moment. She had trusted that she was safe and that someone was there, caring for her, but suddenly that trust was shattered and she was alone, just as she had been after her father died, or when she woke from one of her reveries in which he was still alive.

Matt started to get defensive. "But I was listening. Just because I was doing something with my hands doesn't mean I didn't hear you," I interrupted him. "That's not the issue right now. There'll be time enough to sort out right and wrong later. Right now you have an opportunity to find out something about Julie, something she really needs you to know."

"I just need to know you're not going to leave me, that you'll be there for me when I need you."

Matt was silent for a while. "I thought you were going to leave me. I thought you had decided I wasn't good enough for you."

Julie looked at Matt for a long time. Her face was softer than it had been in many weeks. Her unconscious mind had been telling her that Matt was an impossible man who would never be there for her and might leave at any minute. Now she was able to see Matt as he really was: afraid, confused, angry, *and* caring.

This was an important moment in Matt and Julie's relationship. It was not a magical transformation: there were to be many periods of renewed anger and renewed hopelessness. They would never go back to the innocent days when they first met. But they now had something to build on, something that helped them understand the pain they caused each other in a different way. Julie had succeeded in hiding her fear of abandonment under a heap of criticism of Matt. Her comment about his breaking the VCR was fairly typical. In the weeks that followed, Matt came to understand why he felt like running away when Julie criticized him. Matt's mother always hid her disappointment behind sarcasm, and through his childhood he saw her vitality gradually give way to bitterness. His unconscious mind told him that that was how it was going to be with Julie. And it told him that the only way to protect himself was to flee, either physically, as he had done the other night, or emotionally, by withdrawing into his own private world.

I continued to see Matt and Julie for about four more months. Understanding why they reacted to each other the way they did enabled Matt and Julie to recover more quickly from their fights, and to have some humor about their situation. As Julie put it in one of our last sessions, "I had become convinced that Matt was just an unavailable rock and that nothing ever really got to him. Now I know the truth—he's really a vulnerable rock." Though their actions had not changed dramatically, the meaning they attached to those actions had changed. They no longer felt that their marriage doomed them to repeat the most painful parts of their childhoods.

Matt and Julie were fortunate. The problems in their relationship led them to a crisis, and they were able to seek help. In longer-term relationships the invisible marriage becomes a tangle of repeated patterns. Many couples are so completely involved in their immediate conflict, be it about money, sex, or the division of housework, that they don't realize they've been having the same fight, with different content, for years—with the same results.

MAKING THE INVISIBLE VISIBLE

When you find yourself caught in the uncertainty and pain of the struggle phase of a relationship, or locked into the stultifying pattern of the accommodation phase, there is a way out. You can become conscious of what your real needs are in the relationship and learn to communicate them clearly. And you can become conscious of who your partner really is, and learn to meet, rather than frustrate, his or her needs.

Making the invisible marriage visible enables you to:

Change Stuck Patterns

Once you understand why you and your partner react the way you do to each other, you can begin to choose a different way of responding. Julie saw Matt's need for a few moments to himself when he got home as evidence that he didn't want to be with her. When, because of her fear, she criticized him, he would frequently "check out" for the rest of the night. Once they were able to understand that what Julie needed was to know that Matt really was interested in being with her and that what Matt needed was a few minutes alone to "put himself together," they were able to work out a compromise. Matt would have some time alone right after work, but then they would spend some time connecting with each other.

Stop Blaming Your Partner

Matt had no idea why Julie had become so angry and critical. In his mind she had just turned out to be a mean, sarcastic nag. He was full of blame toward her for behaving like that. This bitterness prevented him from hearing even her reasonable requests for more contact. When he was able to understand her real concerns he was more able to listen to what she wanted from him.

Stop Blaming Yourself

Matt felt guilty that he didn't want to be around Julie more. He felt that he should try and meet her needs, but despite his intentions he kept pulling away. When he saw how his pulling away was a lifelong pattern of defense against being misunderstood and criticized, he felt much less guilty for the behavior. This, in turn, made him much less defensive and better able to hear Julie's needs.

Learn to Ask for What You Really Need

The real needs in relationship, like Julie's for consistency or Matt's for independence and respect, often remain unconscious. Instead of asking for what you want, you fight a symbolic battle. Once you understand these invisible needs, you can begin to ask for them directly, in a way that your partner can hear.

Learn to Meet Your Partner's Deepest Needs

Understanding your partner's deepest needs makes you want to meet them. Being able to love and help your partner makes you feel good about yourself. When Julie was able to give Matt the time he needed when he got home from work without feeling abandoned, she felt proud of herself.

FOUR QUESTIONS ABOUT RELATIONSHIP: DEEPENING THE INQUIRY

Understanding our own invisible marriage may seem like a daunting task. Here are four questions that lead us toward new perspectives on the unconscious dynamics of our relationship:

1. What do we most deeply want from our partner?
2. What do we most deeply fear will happen to us in a relationship?
3. How do we react when we are hurt or threatened?
4. Why have we fallen into fixed roles and ways of relating to each other?

The answers to these questions may seem obvious on the conscious level—we want love, sex, security; we fear divorce, a lack of intimacy, conflict, and so forth. But on the unconscious level they direct our inquiry to the deepest needs and fears of the self, needs and fears that originated in childhood but continue to have enormous power to this day.

Humans begin life completely dependent on an emotional tie to their caregivers. Even if their physical needs are met, children will not thrive without this tie. The fact that our survival depended on the maintenance of this relationship tie is central to the way we unconsciously view relationships. It explains why we behave in relationships in ways that are often diametrically opposed to what we think we need. For instance, Julie wanted Matt to be more available, but she ended up yelling at him, which only drove him further away. To her unconscious mind, the issue was survival: Matt's withdrawal meant that the relationship tie was in jeopardy, and Julie's rage was similar to the tantrum of a traumatized infant.

Freud's groundbreaking theories about the way the unconscious affects our conscious experience focused on biological drives, primarily those of sex and aggression. The individual was the basic unit of psychological life; the individual mind projected its drive-based needs onto others. By contrast, modern relational theories of psychoanalysis focus on the need to maintain the vital relationship tie while preserving and developing the integrity of the self as the basis for unconscious life.

In the light of these relational theories, a preliminary answer to the first question about what we want in relationship would be: we want to preserve the vital relationship tie, while at the same time being able, within the security of that tie, to develop into a unique individual. The answer to the second question follows: we fear that the tie will be broken, or that the price we have to pay to preserve it will be too high.

The answer to the third question, *How do we react when we are hurt or threatened?* draws upon our understanding of another of Freud's concepts, *defenses*. While Freud felt that most of our defenses were based on a disavowal of sexuality and aggression, other psychoanalytic schools see defenses as attempts to preserve the integrity and coherence of our sense of self in the face of potentially damaging emotional pain.

The answers to these first three questions lie in an understanding of childhood development. Our deepest yearnings, our deepest fears, and our defensive reactions all stem from childhood experiences. In the next chapter we will explore the way these childhood experiences shape our feelings and reactions to our partners.

The answer to the fourth question, *Why have we fallen into fixed roles and ways of relating to each other?* draws upon another area of psychological inquiry: the study of human relationships from a systems point of view. Systems theory challenges what Robert Stolorow and George Atwood, founders of the intersubjective school of psychoanalysis, call "the myth of the isolated mind." From a systems point of view, the way we react to our partner in a relationship cannot be understood by looking at individual issues alone. Both partners are part of a relationship system, and this relationship system develops its own ways of controlling behavior and regulating painful feelings in the relationship. In Chapter 3 we will turn our attention to making sense of the way we behave in relationships. We will see how the repetitive patterns in relationships serve to protect us from emotional pain.

For a couple caught up in immediate problems, childhood issues may seem quite remote. In Part II, "Visible Problems, Invisible Roots," we will take a detailed look at the kinds of problems couples encounter and the role of childhood issues in shaping them. The first three chapters deal with three of the most common patterns of relationships, which we will call scripts: those in which anger predominates, those in which one partner pursues contact and the other avoids it, and those in which both partners are emotionally disengaged. In Chapter 7, we turn our attention to the unconscious factors that control couples' sex lives, and in Chapter 8, we look at the other three issues that couples most commonly have conflict about: money, housework, and in-laws.

Part III focuses on creating positive changes. Chapter 9 discusses how to respond to crises in relationship in a way that brings growth along with the pain. Chapter 10 discusses ways to consciously decide to create a better relationship. In the last chapter we explore the way that a conscious relationship can foster growth and healing for both partners.

2

Growing Up Wounded: Childhood Pain and the Origin of the Invisible Marriage

Don't ask me when I learned love
Don't ask me when I learned fear.
Ask about the size of the rooms
how many lived in them
what else the rooms contained
what whispers of the histories of skin.

ADRIENNE RICH

Human development has traditionally been seen as a journey from dependence toward autonomy and independence. More recently some psychologists have questioned this assumption. Heinz Kohut, founder of the self psychology school of psychoanalysis, saw development as a journey from the early dependency of childhood toward increasingly more mature forms of dependency.[1] The need, say, of a child to be admired for learning to ride a two-wheeled bicycle evolves into the adult's need to feel that his or her triumphs and successes in life are singularly important to his or her spouse.

This shift in the way psychologists view human development is enormously important to our understanding of marriage. It means that we must look to childhood experiences not only to find the origins of our problems in adult relationships, but also to find what we most deeply need from a healthy relationship.

WHAT A CHILD NEEDS TO DEVELOP A HEALTHY SELF

According to Kohut, children will develop a healthy sense of self if early on they have two needs satisfied: (1) a sense of being closely connected to a parent or parent figure who completely understands and protects them; and (2) a sense that their actions and achievements have been seen and appreciated. Kohut called the first a need for *idealizing,* and the second a need for *mirroring.* Kohut used the term *selfobject* to describe these types of needs. I refer to them as *self needs.* After considering the primary self needs that Kohut identified and then some that others have added, we will look at what happens when they are not met.

---

1. In 1984, Kohut wrote, "A move from dependence (symbiosis) to independence (autonomy) in the psychological sphere is no more possible, let alone desirable, than a corresponding move from a life dependent on Oxygen to a life independent of it in the biological sphere."

The Need for Idealizing

A newborn infant does not have much sense of its separate existence. It may have left the womb, but it still feels itself to be psychologically connected to its mother. Although a baby can't articulate its needs, somehow its mother seems to understand them; she
feeds it when it's hungry, changes it when it's wet and uncomfortable. If we look at the way an infant lets itself be held when it is
completely relaxed, the way it perfectly molds its body to the con-
tours of the mother, we can see how we may have felt completely
at one with our own mothers. Attachment and developmental theorists such as John Bowlby and Daniel Stern have focused on these
feelings of deep connection as essential for the mother–infant
bonding process.

Developmentalists use the term *attunement* to describe the
process of interaction between the mother and the infant. Attunement means the mother's ability to discern the infant's nonverbal communication of inner states and respond to it. An infant
whose mother is attuned to it does not feel alone or separate;
he feels that his mother is responding to everything that happens
to him. If there is adequate attunement, the infant will form a
healthy psychological bond with the mother. This bonding is
necessary for the later development of an independent sense of
self. It is paradoxical that the only way we can attain our independence is by having an adequate experience of dependency.
Developmentalists focus on the mother's attunement to the infant because, for most children, this is the first and formative experience, but both parents contribute to the establishment of the
idealizing bond. If there is an adequate level of attunement in the
family, the child experiences his parents as all-powerful and all-
knowing. The term *idealizing* is used to describe this bond because
the child needs to believe in the parents' infinite strength, wisdom, and power.

The need for this idealizing relationship persists into later life.
The 10-year-old who falls off her bike will want a mother who can
find the scrape and begin comforting it without her having to say
where it hurts. And isn't the search for romantic love actually a
quest to find an idealized partner, one who will understand us
perfectly and with whom we can feel completely at one?

In addition to responding to the child's needs and feelings, there are other ways that parents create this idealizing feeling. They use their power to control the child's behavior. For example, by setting limits, they allow the child to feel protected from his own immature impulses and connected to someone who is wiser and more powerful than he is. Many parents have trouble setting limits for their children. They are afraid of thwarting their children's natural impulses. It is helpful to these parents to understand how essential adequate limits are for a child's growing sense of self. As the idealizing bond matures, it develops from the early sense of being protected by our parents into a sense of admiration for them.

The Need for Mirroring

Picture a child who drops a toy on the ground, listens for the bang, and then looks up to his parent for a response. He is saying, in effect, "Look what I did, look how powerful I am, to make such a loud noise!" Children need their caregivers to validate their power and achievements. The child's growing self needs parents who let him know they're watching, and that they take pleasure in his achievements. And though our need for this kind of attention diminishes over the years, we continue to need it all our lives.

The earliest experience a baby has of this validation is the way his mother responds to his facial expressions. His mother smiles when he smiles, frowns when he has a sad expression. That's where the term *mirroring* comes from. It is not just the child's actions that are being mirrored, but also his or her inner emotional world. The mother who smiles when her baby drops the toy isn't saying, "What a delightful noise you just made." She is saying, "I am sharing *your* delight in the noise." This seemingly simple experience is of critical importance for the infant. It forms the basis of an empathic bond between the child and his mother.

Empathy

The *American Heritage Dictionary* defines empathy as "identification with and understanding of another's situation, feelings, and

Table 2–1   Normal Childhood Needs

Need	What Parent Does	What Child Feels	What It Builds
Idealizing	Soothes and protects. Understands without needing to be told. Attuned to child's emotional needs. Sets limits, acts as powerful, protecting figure. Seems heroic to child.	Secure, bonded to caregiver, calm ("help is on the way") protected, important (because connected to important; shine by reflected light).	Healthy self-esteem, healthy dependency; can soothe self in adversity; can admit need for others, give and get love; capacity to have guiding ideals.
Mirroring	Admires and affirms child's achievements. Responds to child's emotions. Listens to his stories. Delights in his independence.	Important, capable, increasingly independent, energized.	Competency, self-worth, healthy independence, creativity, ambition.

motives." Empathy is the ground from which a healthy self grows. A child who feels her parents can identify with her point of view and understand her feelings experiences two essential things: a sense that she is not alone in the universe but is intimately connected to others, and a sense that her thoughts and feelings are comprehensible to another. A child who grows up in an empathic environment learns to trust her own thoughts and feelings, and she learns to risk reaching out to others with her aliveness and creativity.

Empathy continues to be an essential ingredient in adult relationships. Virtually all the problems I see in marriages involve a breakdown of empathy, which leads to a disruption of the relationship tie. Instead of saying to each other, "I can understand why you would see things that way or do what you do," couples in trouble say to each other, directly or indirectly, "There is something defective and incomprehensible about your feelings and actions." Reestablishing and deepening empathy is the most important work a couple can do. In Part III, we will look at specific ways couples can build or rebuild an empathic connection.

Both idealizing and mirroring experiences build empathy. Together they create an environment in which the child feels both understood and responded to.

Twinship

Kohut described a third experience that is vital to healthy self-development. Kohut called this need the *alter ego* or *twinship* self-object experience. It is the need for having someone else who is enough like you that you don't feel like a stranger, alone in the universe. The power of the twinship experience can be seen in the effectiveness of self-help groups such as Alcoholics Anonymous. Just coming into such a group and finding others with problems and experiences like yours can be a powerful healing experience.

The twinship experience is also an important part of marriage. Though heterosexual partners are obviously different in a basic way, they still look to each other for a sense of identity in such areas as values, goals, and beliefs. When one partner changes dramatically, the other can feel traumatized by the sudden removal of this sense of twinship.

Other Self Needs

Kohut's followers have added their own ideas of self needs. Two that I find particularly useful in understanding what couples need from each other are the *self-delineating experience* and the experience of having *emotional injuries named and repaired.*

The self-delineating experience, defined by Robert Stolorow, Bernard Brandchaft and George Atwood is best understood in terms of what it provides. In the presence of self-delineating experiences, the child develops a sense of the reality of his own thoughts and feelings. To use a popular term, he feels *grounded.* Idealizing and mirroring experiences create a powerful sense of connection and identity between the child and his parents, but from earliest infancy the parent also communicates that the child is unique and separate. In the presence of this affirmation of his separateness, the child develops a healthy sense of boundaries between himself and other people; he knows where he leaves off and another person begins.

The concept of the self-delineating experience is useful in understanding adult relationships in two ways. First, it gives us insight into one of the things that couples most want from each other: validation of their own experience. Many times couples get into desperate battles about who is right and who is wrong about a particular issue. Each is fighting for a self-delineating experience that will acknowledge the reality of his or her experience. The tragedy is that they have created a situation in which only one person can get it. One of the main interventions of therapy is to help the couple learn to acknowledge that both of their subjective experiences can be valid.

When a child does not develop a healthy sense of his own reality, his ability to have intimate relationships as an adult will be limited. He may be so hungry for confirmation of his reality that any difference with his partner will be painful, or he might be so fearful of having his sense of reality threatened that he will avoid intimacy altogether.

The idea that the naming and repairing of emotional injuries is so important in self-development that it deserves to be called a self-object need was suggested by Dr. Jeffrey Trop, a leading theorist of the intersubjective school. This self need is closely related to the self-delineating one. When parents don't acknowledge the pain their actions cause a child, a vital part of the child's reality goes unacknowledged. The absence of a secondary response from parents that acknowledges a child's hurt feelings can often be more damaging than the injury itself. This is especially true in families where there is denial of a problem such as alcoholism or mental illness. A child in such a family will grow to doubt the validity of his own painful feelings. In adult relationships, he will have difficulty defending himself or demanding that his partner change hurtful behaviors. On the other hand, when a parent acknowledges a child's hurt feelings, he is teaching the child both that his experiences are valid and that his tie to the parent can be restored when it is disrupted. This experience will enable him to withstand injuries and resolve conflicts in adult relationships. If a conflict ensues, he will know that all is not lost, and will be more likely to seek acknowledgment of his feelings from his partner, rather than blame or punish her.

TWO WAY INFLUENCE:
THEORIES OF MUTUAL REGULATION

One of the most interesting findings of modern infant development research is that babies train their mothers in how to take care of them. When a mother meets her child's needs she is responding to cues the baby gives her: body language, facial expression, tone, and speed of the child's activity. The baby then responds to the mother's activity of holding, rocking, soothing, and tickling. So intertwined are the two that the British psychoanalyst and pediatrician D. W. Winnicott believed that, in our understanding of child development, there was no such thing as a baby alone. The unit of a baby and a mother is indivisible.

Later Developmentalists such as Daniel Stern and Beatrice Beebe use the phrase *system of mutual regulation* to describe the complex web of mother–child interactions. The child regulates the mother—bringing her out of her distractions when he needs attention, looking away when he does not want attention—and the mother regulates the infant—soothing him when he is agitated, stimulating him to bring him more into the relationship. Most of the time this mutual regulation happens seamlessly and unconsciously, but the result is crucial for the child's developing sense of self. From inside the safety of his ongoing connection with his mother, the child develops the sense of what it's like to be in relationship. If all goes well, he not only learns that he has a separate self and that his need for separateness and privacy can be respected, but also that his deepest needs are knowable and that they can be met by another. Perhaps most importantly, he learns to trust the process of mutual regulation: if things are not going well, if he and his mother are out of tune, they will eventually come back to a way of being together that meets his needs.

The notion of unconscious mutual regulation is very important for our understanding of adult intimate relationships. Like a mother and a child, the partners in a relationship are continually responding to subtle cues that convey the other's needs for intimacy or separateness. Let's take a simple example: a wife is listening to music and doing the dishes. Her husband, attracted to this lively scene, comes up behind her and hugs her. Startled out of her pleasant reverie, she pushes him away. He goes and gets the sports page. The wife, sensing his hurt, smiles at him, throws him a dish towel, and suggests that he dry.

This is an example of a successful mutual regulation. But often couples are not so successful. One possibility is that the slightest misunderstandings cannot be regulated and escalate into a major conflict. Another possibility, as we will see in the next chapter, is that these mutual regulation interactions develop over time into stereotypical ways of relating that I call *scripts*. A simple cue, such as the wife's rebuff of her husband's hug, is enough to trigger a series of predictable and repetitive interactions. These scripts regulate the feelings in relationship, but only at the expense of spontaneity.

PROBLEMS IN SELF DEVELOPMENT: ABANDONMENT AND INTRUSION

We can use the self needs perspective on development to address the question of what we most fear will happen to us in a relationship.

A healthy self must be able to initiate action on its own behalf, and it also must be able to take solace, help, and security from others. If we don't get enough mirroring, or if we don't have parents who foster our idealization, we may grow up unable to maintain our individuality, or unable to be dependent enough to let others nourish us. Children experience their parents' failure to meet their self needs as *abandonment* (when parents are emotionally unavailable) or *intrusion* (when parents are too needy or controlling to let their children separate).

Abandonment

Sometimes a parent isn't present enough, physically or emotionally, for the child to develop a healthy sense of dependence and security. This creates a feeling of *abandonment*. Abandonment feelings can originate from an actual separation, such as a serious illness that requires hospitalization either of the child or the parent, or when a parent is preoccupied or not adequately attuned to the child's emotional reality. The child of an alcoholic, for instance, would certainly feel abandoned when her parent was too drunk to notice her, even though he or she was physically present. A child also feels abandoned when a parent lacks empathy for her emotional reality. A parent who gets angry at a very young child for not being able to stop crying, for instance, has little understanding of a young child's poor ability to control her emotions.

Abandonment feelings also arise when parents are insecure and convey their insecurity to their children. Parents who are overly anxious or who have psychological problems of their own may be unable to convey a sense of comfort and security to their children. Imagine a child who has a minor injury, such as a cut knee. Instead of calming her, her nervous mother says, "I told you rollerskating was dangerous." Rather than providing the needed mirroring response, the mother builds herself up by expressing her own rightness. Of course, all parents respond like this some of the time. It is only when these responses predominate that long-term feelings of abandonment ensue. Whatever their origin, abandonment feelings can be very traumatic, because the child's very survival depends on the maintenance of the parent–child tie.

Intrusion

There are also parents who are unable to appreciate or tolerate their child's moves toward independence. They may themselves feel abandoned as their child becomes more separate. To ward off such feelings, they may be overly controlling, or treat the child as an extension of their own thoughts and feelings. The old joke about a parent telling her child, "I'm cold, go put a coat on" is a good example of this. This kind of *intrusion* is very damaging to a child's growing sense of independence.

Intrusive parents place conditions on providing a self-delineating experience for the child. They say, in effect, I will only acknowledge those parts of you that are like me or that I need from you. Some parents project their own fears onto a child. For example, a mother who herself fears men might refuse to allow her daughter to date or socialize. There is also the more subtle intrusion of a parent who sees his child's achievements as too much of a reflection of himself. Imagine how intruded upon a son feels slinking away from his father's overzealous cheering at a Little League game. Overly strict parents are also intrusive. Strict parents often fear their own spontaneity, and so try to control their child's exuberance.

To a certain extent all parents intrude on their children. But a child whose parents are constantly trying to compensate for their own frustrations by living through him, or whose parents project their own fears or controlling impulses onto him, will come to feel that nothing he does is really just for himself. And his sense of self, his ability to say, "This is me," "This is what I've done," "This is what I like," will not develop properly. As adults, children who were severely intruded on face a constant dilemma. They want to maintain a relationship tie to their partner, but feel that the only way to do that is to deny or suppress their own thoughts and feelings.

I have discussed abandonment and intrusion as separate experiences for the sake of clarity, but children whose parents are extremely intrusive will also feel abandoned. A physically abusive mother is not only being overly controlling, she is also grossly unattuned to her child's feelings of pain and terror. Similarly, children whose parents are always after them to meet their own needs will feel not only intruded upon, but also alone, as if no one is there just for them.

Abandonment and intrusion experiences happen to all of us in childhood. No child is unscathed by painful experiences of loneliness, frustration, and anger. Every child has experiences similar to those of 10-year-old Timmy, whose deepest wish was to go to sports camp with his friends, but whose overly fearful mother told him, "I'm not having you come home with your foot in a cast or your arm in a sling." Everyone has had abandonment experiences like those of a client of mine named Lisa, who bitterly remembers her mother talking to a friend all through her piano recital. Problems arise only when such experiences are so pervasive that they overshadow all other emotions.

Shame

Shame is a third experience, in addition to abandonment and intrusion, that negatively affects a child's self development. Children who grow up feeling a lot of shame learn to hide their real thoughts and feelings behind nearly impermeable defenses. Shame is one of the most powerful and destructive feelings there is. Unlike guilt, which is the feeling that we have *done* something wrong, shame is the feeling that something is *wrong with us*. Shame adds a vicious twist to experiences of abandonment and intrusion. In addition to the pain these experiences cause by themselves, children who grow up ashamed do not feel that they are worthy of having a reliable connection or of having their separateness respected. Shame involves the fear that our defectiveness will be exposed to the world. Let me briefly summarize what psychologists know about the origin and effect of this powerful emotion:

Shame has its origin in a failure of mirroring. The child's natural exuberance and excitement is met with indifference or criticism by his parent. Of course, no parent can match his or her child's excitement all the time, and criticism is often necessary to correct a child's behavior. But when criticism or indifference become the predominant reaction, the child grows ashamed of his own excitement.

In order to make sense of being repeatedly rejected or criticized, children come to blame themselves. They feel that they don't deserve attention or admiration, and they become ashamed of their need for it.

Since shame involves a fear of being exposed, children who grow up feeling ashamed of themselves learn to hide their needs in various ways. They may become emotionally closed and withdrawn, or they may become angry and rebellious. Some children become perfectionists and critical of both themselves and others. Still others pursue a "best defense is a good offense" plan and constantly seek attention. The class clown is a good example of this.

Whatever the defense against shame, the result is the same. The aspirations and yearnings of the real self become hidden.

SHAME IN RELATIONSHIPS

Since shame is such a painful emotion, most of us want to avoid it at all costs. And since shame involves a fear of being exposed, intimate relationships pose a great threat—the partners develop a whole range of techniques for hiding their selves from each other and, indeed, from themselves as well. Here are some examples of the way shame distorts couple relationships:

Men and Women Disavowing Their Needs

In our society, shame is often gender-related. Little boys are taught not to cry or act needy, while girls are taught to act "lady-like" and not show off. As a result, boys grow up ashamed of their dependency needs and girls grow up ashamed of their needs to have their achievements and excitement mirrored. So, relationships are often stereotyped. The man feels safe only when asserting his needs for separateness and admiration for his accomplishments, and the woman feels safe only when asserting her needs for closeness and understanding. Of course we all need *both* idealizing and mirroring experiences. In Chapter 5 we will look at relationships in which the woman pursues contact and the man avoids it.

Hiding Behind Conflict

Conflict around basic needs hides the shame we may feel about dependency. Instead of letting our needs, which we are ashamed of, show, we pick a fight. This gives us simultaneously contact and protection from exposure. It's easier for the man who felt humiliated at work to come home and say, "This place is a mess," than it is to say, "Boy, do I need someone to talk to who will understand me tonight."

No Surprises, Please

Intimate relationships present us with feelings of excitement and opportunities to act in new, spontaneous ways, but since a key component of shame is the fear of being surprised or found out, our defenses do not allow us to act spontaneously. In relationships our defenses protect us by leading us to predictable patterns of interaction and stifling excitement.

Delegating Incompetence

When one partner acts irresponsibly, the other partner, by contrast, feels competent and in control. The irresponsible partner carries the shame for both of them. This is the classic codependency scenario.

Avoiding Sex

Shame is very much a body feeling. Children feel their excitement in their bodies. If that excitement meets with constant disapproval, they become ashamed of their bodies. One of the things we seek in a sexual relationship is a chance to reexperience that childlike excitement in our body in a loving and approving atmosphere. But there's a risk: if we surrender to these feelings we might find that our partner rejects them. Frequently at the beginning of the relationship, when there is no history of rejection, sex goes well. But eventually little misunderstandings or failures accrue and reinforce the feelings of shame that one or both partners have about their sexuality. As a result the couple develops a sexual routine designed to protect them from feeling ashamed of their physical excitement. We will return to the issue of sex in relationships in Chapter 7.

SHELTER FROM THE STORM: HOW WE RESPOND TO ABANDONMENT, INTRUSION, AND SHAME

As children, our responses to emotional pain, such as feelings of abandonment, shame, or intrusion, were largely controlled by our autonomic nervous systems. This is the part of the nervous system that is governed by our unconscious mind. It is the so-called "old" brain that resembles an animal's, and its purpose is purely defensive. When threatened, it knows only two basic reactions: fight or flight. An animal will either growl or flee when it feels its survival is threatened. A child whose needs are frustrated will either express rage or flee into a comforting fantasy.

The form of fight or flight that a child uses to defend himself against emotional pain can be very complex. Whereas an animal has only two choices—bare its fangs or hightail it—human responses to an emotional threat are much more varied and subtle. The flight response, rather than involving physical running, can be an emotional withdrawal, a retreat into a fantasy world where the child has perfect parents who appreciate him because he is a superhero. It is no coincidence that 3- and 4-year-olds' penchant for donning capes and pretending to be Batman comes at just the developmental time when they are terribly vulnerable to feelings that their parents are being too strict or are not mirroring their accomplishments.

One way to understand the flight defense is to look at the way it stays with us into adulthood. Adults often flee from emotional pain into a comforting fantasy—a daydream, for example, in which we meet someone who will appreciate us. Addictive behavior is also a type of flight defense. Faced with a painful situation, we withdraw into a fantasy of fulfillment through food or alcohol. Compulsive behavior, such as becoming a workaholic, is also a flight from emotional pain, as is depression, which is a withdrawal of life energy from the world.

The fight response can be equally complex. It may mean yelling and screaming, but it can just as easily mean a stubborn battle of noncompliance. The child who didn't get appreciated enough may try to fight his parents by stubbornly refusing to achieve anything at all. His fight response becomes an "all right then, I'll show you" attitude. Or the child may appear to comply with the parents' wishes while secretly resisting. He will agree to do the dishes but then find excuses to postpone starting. This is the passive-aggressive style of relating, which involves being overtly compliant, in order to avoid an open confrontation, while at the same time being covertly defiant of the other person's requests or expectations.

Another way children handle the fight response is to turn it inward, against themselves. Faced with the danger of feeling rage at a parent, which can be a terrifying feeling for a young child, he learns to direct the anger toward himself. Let's take an example of a child who has overly critical parents. The child brings home a pretty good report card, but his parents only notice the one bad grade. The child cannot say, "I hate the way you only notice the negative things about me." He needs to believe that his parents are wise and are looking after him, so instead he will direct his anger or fight response inward and say to himself, "I messed up, I must really be worthless." If this pattern continues, eventually the child tells himself that "I'll just never be good enough." This has devastating effects on his self-esteem.

THE REAL SELF AND THE DEFENSIVE SELF

If emotional nourishment is adequate, the new self grows up straight and proud like a tree. But if nourishment is lacking, or the self meets with an obstacle it must grow around, it will grow up bent or distorted like a shrub. D. W. Winnicott coined the term *real self* for the self that receives enough nourishment to grow up straight, and the term *false self* for the one that grows up responding to an obstacle in its path. Because the goal of safety is not really false, I call it the *defensive self*.

The real self is the seat of plans, creativity, and authentic feelings. When we feel competent and proud of our accomplishments, we are in the realm of the real self. When we feel seen and understood by another, when someone really knows "where we're coming from," they are touching our real self.

The defensive self acts like a protective shell around the real self. A familiar example of the defensive self in action is the "sour grapes" attitude. In order to protect the real self from disappointment, the defensive self says, "I didn't really want those grapes anyway." Its function is to keep the real self out of harm's way. The defensive self teaches us to avoid repeating mistakes and getting hurt again. A child who proudly shows a parent a painting and meets with a bored or critical response will feel disappointed. And if this response is repeated again and again, the defensive self begins to develop. The child will learn to stop wanting his creation to be seen. He may start telling himself that he really doesn't like to paint anyway. Eventually he will flee from his own feelings of pride or desire for attention.

No one knows why some children tend to flee from emotional pain while others tend to fight. Perhaps there is a subtle process of trial and error until the child learns what works best in his or her own family. Either way, the defensive self's job is to protect the real self from suffering an injurious experience ("We're not

Table 2–2   Defensive Strategies

Response to	Flight	Fight
Abandonment	Depressed, withdrawn, fantasies of perfect partner, addictions	Angry, hysterical, clinging or pursuing, critical
Intrusion	Isolated, emotionally unavailable, compulsive, workaholic, intellectualizes.	Angry, violent, withholding, passive-aggressive, exhibitionistic.

going to go through this again"). Most of us can identify with one or more of these defensive strategies and with how our typical responses to emotional pain or stress, such as yelling or eating or working compulsively, actually derive from our childhood experiences. But why would the defensive styles we learned back then persist? To answer that we must look at the way the unconscious mind is capable of confusing the past and the present.

TRANSFERENCE: THE TIME MACHINE

Let's recall the incident between Matt and Julie from the last chapter that led to their terrible fight. Julie has been telling Matt about her first day of actually working as a nurse. She looks up to see him fiddling with the toaster, apparently not listening, and says, "Put that thing down. You already broke the VCR last week." Then Matt, without a word, turns and walks out of the room.

On the surface, Matt's reaction seems pretty straightforward: Julie said something that annoyed him, and he walked away to show his displeasure. But if we look at his reaction from the perspective of the unconscious mind, where memories of childhood intrusion and abandonment are stored, we see a different picture.

The unconscious mind works by matching patterns of behavior and response. It does not matter if the original pattern happened twenty-five or even fifty years ago. To the unconscious mind, all time is the present. Notice how time can be confused in dreams, for example, where the subject may be our present family but the setting is our childhood house. Matt's unconscious mind matched the pattern of Julie turning her frustration into criticism of his competency with memories of his mother doing the same thing. When the match was made, Julie became identical with his mother.

Psychologists use the term *transference* to describe this confusion of past people and experiences with the present. The term derives from therapy, where patients project their past experiences, especially with their parents, onto the therapist.

Matt's transference led his defensive self to take over and, without thinking about it, he fled from the scene. In fact, Matt's unconscious mind had gone to work even before Julie's angry comment. It picked up Julie's excitement about her day and her anxiety about how Matt was going to respond, and matched it with memories of how his mother's neediness intruded on him. This is why he was fiddling with the toaster in the first place: he had withdrawn into his private world of thinking about mechanical objects and how they work.

The unconscious mind compares every new emotional experience to a pre-existing pattern of disappointments and psychological traumas. Faced with a new emotional experience, such as "My husband's late," the unconscious mind matches it with a preexisting pattern, such as "My parents used to leave me alone to cry as an infant." Finding this match, the defensive self initiates a fight response ("You s.o.b., dinner's ruined") or a flight response ("I'd better have a cigarette," or "My old boyfriend Bill would never have treated me like this").

Sometimes there really is a threat in our emotional world that requires the defensive self's protection. For instance, as Elisabeth Kubler-Ross and others have pointed out, denial, or a temporary fleeing from overwhelming reality, is a normal and necessary stage in the grieving process. When someone close to us dies, our defensive self's pattern matching function identifies a real emotional threat and initiates a life-preserving defensive reaction so that we can continue to function.

Other times the matching function produces an overreaction. The wife who yells at her husband for being late is not really threatened with abandonment. Her unconscious mind is reacting to the *similarity* of his lateness to her memory of childhood pain. The husband who yells at his wife for misplacing his tools is not actually so upset about having to look for a screwdriver. Instead he's upset because his unconscious mind has matched this event with times in his childhood when his parents refused to respect his privacy or leave his possessions—symbols of his budding identity—alone.

Our understanding of the defensive self gives us an answer to our third relationship question, *How do we react when hurt or threatened?* Our reactions to emotional pain, especially when it is based in transference, are controlled by the defensive self, which unconsciously initiates coping strategies that we learned in childhood.

GOOD ENOUGH PARENTING

No one has perfect parents. No one has parents who understood their every need, and no one has parents who appreciated their every achievement. No child grows up without pain and psychological injury. A child who grew up in perfect innocence would be totally unadapted to the real world, which is full of emotional and physical threats. D. W. Winnicott used the term *good enough parenting* to indicate some kind of minimum level of parental function that provides the basis for healthy self development. But no one has ever been able to quantify such parenting, or even accurately account for the fact that some children come through seemingly horrendous childhoods with a relatively intact sense of self, and others come through much less traumatic experiences with an overfunctioning defensive self and an underdeveloped real self.

With the exception of those who suffered extreme trauma or abuse, most people could not say they had absolutely bad parents. Most of us had enough mirroring and idealizing experiences to develop a healthy sense of self, and enough failures or traumas to also have developed an active defensive self that leaves us ever ready to flee from reality or hide behind our anger.

In our adult life, we have areas where our real self functions quite well and areas where we are stuck responding defensively when our self is threatened. In relationships we express our true feelings one time and react in an automatic, defensive manner the next. The wife who flies off the handle when her husband is late may be able at another time to calmly say, "John, I really need you to stop reading the newspaper and listen to me."

The self is not a fixed entity, but one that changes all the time. When we are under stress or have suffered a series of losses or setbacks, we are more likely to be sensitive to emotional threats. If we have recently had our self recharged by being appreciated or understood by our partner, we may be able to overlook the next evocation of abandonment or intrusion. But certain actions so resemble a painful childhood scenario that they will almost always trigger a defensive response.

DEALING WITH CORE ISSUES IN RELATIONSHIPS

The things that "push our buttons" invariably touch core issues. They are the wounds of abandonment, intrusion, or shame the self carries into adulthood. Matt's reaction to the slightest criticism from Julie reflects the core issue of his mother's critical intrusiveness. Core issues are like the mammoth frozen in ice in a science fiction tale. When the ice melts the mammoth emerges fully alive. The end of the "ice age" comes when we enter into an intimate relationship.

In order to stop reacting defensively in a relationship, we must be able to understand the core issues that create those defensive reactions. This process involves looking back into childhood and honestly examining what went wrong, which can be a painful experience because it means punching through defenses and denial. We may be reluctant to blame our parents, who did the best they could, or we may be reluctant to relive painful experiences that now seem far behind us.

Many people feel that there is a distinction between working on themselves and working on their relationship. They may even feel that they have to resolve their core issues before they can have a successful relationship. I disagree. I think relationships offer the best opportunity we have to change defensive patterns and resolve our core issues. After all, relationships bring these issues to the surface again. Plus, it is much easier to relive painful experiences if you know you have the support of a loving partner than it is to relive them alone. Finding someone who will mirror and appreciate our individuality can undo a core issue of abandonment and help heal a hurt self.

To work on a relationship at this level takes a great deal of courage and commitment. But as we shall see in the next chapter, the alternative is to settle for a pattern of relating that merely keeps childhood beasts frozen.

3

Patterns
of Protection

So, lovers dreame a rich and long delight
But get a winter-seeming summers night.

JOHN DONNE

As we saw in the last chapter, each of us enters into adult relationships with two distinct parts of our self left over from childhood: a real self that seeks understanding and appreciation from our partner, and a defensive self that seeks to avoid reexperiencing core issues of intrusion, abandonment, and shame.

One would think that this combination would lead us into a relationship that would, in the words of an old song, "accentuate the positive" and "eliminate the negative." The person who felt abandoned as a child would seek someone constant and giving, while the person who felt intruded on would seek someone strong and independent.

Unfortunately, it rarely works out that way. In fact, as we shall see in a moment, it often works out just the opposite way. Instead of the "rich and long delight" that we dream of, most often we end up with a relationship that neither meets all of our needs nor leaves us mortally wounded. Most relationships are neither as desolate as John Donne's "winter-seeming" night nor as warm and summery as we yearn for. In fact, the function of the invisible marriage is to protect us from the emotional ravages of winter while at the same time keeping alive the hope that despite the current "cold" the heat of earlier passion will return.

In this chapter we will look at how two people, drawn together by their yearnings for closeness and pulled apart by their fear of getting hurt, develop a relationship *system*, and how this system eventually takes on a life of its own, outside of their conscious control. This relationship system works to protect them from pain, while at the same time keeping alive the hope that the real self's needs will eventually be met. We will also come to understand what I call the *paradox of protection*: that a constant, predictable pattern of pain or frustration in a relationship often protects the partners from a deeper or less well-known pain.

FROM EXCITEMENT TO FAMILIARITY

Most people seem to choose mates based on two contradictory principles: excitement and familiarity. On the one hand, we say to ourselves, "This person may meet needs I've never had met before." On the other hand, we say, "This is known territory, I can handle this." At an unconscious level, the seeming contradiction is easily explained: the yearning for excitement and difference represents the real self's hopes for fulfillment, and the need for familiarity represents the defensive self's fear that a new or unpredictable relationship will bring new trauma.

During the honeymoon phase, the real self's long-buried needs for understanding and appreciation reappear. New lovers seem to talk in a code or private language, as if they understand each other perfectly. New lovers can't wait to share their daily experiences with each other; they're sure their partners will be as excited as they are about their successes or as sad as they are about their disappointments. Sometimes the intoxication of love is so powerful that it lulls the defensive self into a kind of slumber. "Don't worry," Love whispers to the real self, "this is finally it, at long last the authentic you can come out and be perfectly safe."

But the defensive self is not really asleep. It is right there being vigilant. Inevitably one partner forgets to call and the other feels abandoned, or one partner begins to feel uncomfortably intruded on by the assumption, prevalent among couples, that they should think and act alike. At that point, the sleeping defensive self may wake with a start. This is particularly true if the unconscious mind has matched an incident of abandonment or intrusion with a core issue left over from childhood. Then we begin to fear that the honeymoon phase, in which we come to expect to get core needs met, might lead not to a second chance but to a second trauma.

When the defensive self gets its wake-up call, relationships enter a period of testing, struggle, and uncertainty. Tests and symbolic battles over issues of abandonment and intrusion predominate: "If I plan a special dinner, will he be there on time?" "If I want to watch this football game, will she interrupt me?" This testing leads to resentment: "You never doubted my loyalty to you before. How come you're making a federal case over my being fifteen minutes late?"

The word *familiar* comes from the root word *family*. Out of the chaos of the power-struggle phase, the defensive self begins reacting as it did in childhood. If our childhood defense was to fight, we grow angry. If our childhood defense was to flee, we begin to withdraw. The relationship recreates a familiar pattern: our partner becomes our parent, and we react as we did as children. Let's look at an example of how this pattern evolves.

LARRY AND ROXANNE

Larry and Roxanne met in college. He was a star basketball player and she was a cheerleader. The first couple of years of their relationship resembled a storybook romance. Roxanne went to Larry's games, and after his practices they would go out to dinner and talk about their respective days. Larry had hoped for a professional contract when they graduated. When this didn't materialize, he decided to play in Spain. Roxanne went with him, and they spent the first year of their marriage traveling constantly, living in tiny rooms. It was very tough, but they were happy. This honeymoon phase had particular meaning for both of them. They both were getting something that had been lacking in their childhoods.

Larry was the oldest of five children. His was a very traditional Eastern European family, and as the oldest child he was expected to be responsible for the other siblings. Moreover, his mother suffered from manic depression. Larry's father minimized her illness and withdrew when she entered an acute phase, leaving Larry to pinch-hit. "My brothers got to play all they wanted to," Larry told me, "but although my mother would promise that I could go out to the park, at the last minute she would change her mind and find something for me to do around the house." Larry's real job was keeping his mother company when she was depressed. This he did dutifully, repressing his resentment.

When he got a sports scholarship to go away to college, he felt released from his mother's intrusion. And when he met Roxanne, who seemed delighted when he played ball, and who shared his successes and failures, Larry felt that he would finally get the consistent mirroring he never had as a child.

Roxanne was also very tied to her mother, but rather than feel intruded on by her neediness, she felt rejected by her criticism. Roxanne's mother was displeased with her distant and critical husband, and she took her disappointment out on her children. The children took different defensive paths against their mother's demands and criticisms. Roxanne's sister became rebellious; Roxanne tried to be perfect. "I would spend hours on my clothes and hair when I was in high school, but my mother would always find something to pick apart." She turned her anger at her mother's criticism against herself and became a relentless perfectionist.

Roxanne also had a difficult time with her father. He would give her what she called "his silent treatment" when he disapproved of her. "We would be playing, having a good time, and all of a sudden, it's like a switch would go off, and he would just stop talking to me."

Roxanne was very attracted to Larry's oldest-child dutifulness. He was sensitive to her moods and listened to her when she talked. She was also attracted to his star status on campus. It looked then as if her idealizing needs were going to be met, that she had finally found someone who would make her feel understood and safe.

The End of the Honeymoon

At the end of their year in Spain, Larry and Roxanne had to decide where they were going to live and what they were going to do. Rather then decide openly, Larry just assumed that they would move back to his hometown, where he had a job waiting for him in the athletic department of a local junior college. Roxanne swallowed her misgivings and went along with him.

Their honeymoon phase ended almost immediately after this move. Roxanne sensed that being around his parents brought out a different side of Larry. "He stopped being the happy, loving guy I married. He grew quiet, and he started spending most of his time at his parents' house." Larry had resumed his family role of being the dutiful son. Roxanne, who was having trouble finding a job in her chosen profession, began to feel abandoned, and she began to feel that her own needs didn't count. Of course, these two feelings matched very well with memories of her relationship with her parents. Her usual defense of trying to be perfect—in this case, trying to appear happy and in control—just signaled to Larry that everything was all right. When Roxanne grew more depressed and began increasing her demands on Larry's time, he dismissed her as just upset because she had not found a job yet. However, when she did find a job, she was still not happy.

At this point, Larry's own defensive alarms went off. He made a match between Roxanne's unhappiness and his mother's depression. This was very confusing to Larry. He knew that his responsibility was to take care of a needy woman, but he unconsciously resented the intrusion. Outwardly he tried to be helpful—he supported Roxanne in her job search, and tried to introduce her to his friends—but at the same time he began withdrawing into sullen silences. And when he did communicate, he picked at her for being too uptight and demanding.

Recreating Childhood Issues

It began to seem that their worst fears had come true. Larry saw Roxanne as overly sensitive, angry, and needy, while Roxanne saw Larry as unreliable and critical. They were right back where they had started, reliving the most painful aspects of their childhoods.

Was this some perverse stroke of fate? I have seen it happen too many times in couples to think so. The partners in virtually every relationship see each other through this transference at least some of the time, and most eventually develop themes and conflicts in their relationships that recreate their childhoods. This leads us to two important questions: (1) Why do these transference feelings take on a life of their own? and (2) How do individuals seeking mates from the pool of millions of possible choices manage to find partners who resemble their parents enough to evoke this transference?

Let's tackle the first question. There are three reasons why we come to reenact a childhood scenario:

1. *It's familiar.* The Scandinavian immigrants who settled in Minnesota could have settled in more temperate regions, but instead they opted for land that reminded them of home—they

knew how to handle land like that. Familiarity allows us to use the defensive strategies that we learned as children. The woman who survived an angry parent by living in a fantasy world might choose an angry partner in order to have an opportunity to "zone out" as she did when she was a child. There's more of a risk in seeking a new experience than in surviving a familiar, if painful, one. Psychoanalyst Bernard Brandchaft has a wonderful phrase for describing the preference for a known pain over an unknown possibility. He calls it "the dread *not* to repeat."

2. *It's the best we think we deserve.* As explained in the last chapter, children blame themselves for childhood trauma. They feel ashamed of the needs that did not get met. If we were abandoned as a child, we will feel that that is what we deserve as an adult. If we come from a very intrusive family, we will not feel entitled to have a mate who will respect our need for privacy.

3. *It's where the action is.* Freud coined the term *repetition compulsion* for the way his patients seemed to reenact painful circumstances. Later theorists have come to see the process as a sign of promise. Our unconscious minds guide us to relationships that replicate childhood experiences because that is where we find the issues we need to master in life. It's as if such relationships were offering us a second chance: "So you never learned how to set limits with your mother? Well, here's your chance to do it with your wife." "So you never learned how to stand up to your father when he put you down? Well, here's a chance to learn to be more assertive with your husband."

For Roxanne, merely stating her disappointment to Larry in couples therapy was taking a step beyond her childhood, when the best she could do was to try to be even more perfect. For Larry, complaining to Roxanne that she was being too uptight and controlling was a step toward breaking out of the dutiful son role.

Now, let's turn to the second question: how do we manage to find a partner with whom to act out these childhood scenarios? Again, there are three main ways:

1. *We choose a mate who is like our parents.* Sometimes this is obvious, such as when the child of an alcoholic marries someone

who has an obvious drinking problem. But it's not always so obvious. Although Roxanne thought she had chosen a man who was the exact opposite of her parents, somehow her defensive self detected that underneath Larry's easygoing manner he had the potential to be angry, critical, and withdrawn. This is not really as mysterious as it sounds. As a child I was very afraid of one of my uncles. He used to throw me up in the air and wrestle with me. It looked like fun, but I could tell that there was a slight mean streak in him. Roxanne's sixth sense saw Larry's other side and, rather than repel her, it was one of the things that attracted her to him.

2. *We respond selectively to our partner's behavior.* Larry behaved in a number of different ways after the move back to his home town. He began spending more time with his parents. He also took an active interest in Roxanne's job search. But Roxanne's defensive self perceived in Technicolor those things he did that reminded her of her parents; she saw the other behaviors in black and white. She reacted angrily to the things that made her feel abandoned, while ignoring Larry's attempts to be caring or helpful.

3. *We project our fears onto our partner.* Eventually, all the "evidence" that our defensive self gathers by responding selectively to our partner convinces us that our partner is really "guilty" of abandonment or intrusion. This projection makes those fears come true. When Roxanne's defensive self decided that Larry was going to abandon her, she began pushing him away. Once Larry realized that Roxanne had decided that he was a man who couldn't be trusted, a part of him gave up trying to please her. Of course, he still went through the motions, just as he had with his mother. This only confirmed Roxanne's determination not to trust him anymore.

Withholding

One of the first things partners do in the face of emotional peril is they begin to pull back from meeting each other's needs. Of course, this is in part retaliation for the hurt they are causing each other. Retaliatory withholding seeks to communicate a feeling, and at least potentially carries a promise: "Treat me better and I'll meet your self needs again."

But partners also begin withholding for reasons that are largely unconscious and more purely defensive. In the honeymoon phase, each partner's ability to meet the other's needs was part of the expansive joy. Roxanne was delighted to go to Europe with Larry and to mirror his athletic accomplishments; for the first time in her life she didn't have to live in the emotionally restricted world of her family. Now, seeing him shut down around his family, she was less willing to mirror his ambitions, not just to punish him, but also because she had herself contracted emotionally. The spontaneous, loving expression of her real self now felt dangerous.

This kind of contraction affects both partners in the marriage system; it resets the emotional thermostat from warm to cool. Even though Roxanne was just protecting herself, Larry felt injured and began to withhold from meeting her self needs to protect himself. This mutually induced withholding marked the end of Larry and Roxanne's prolonged honeymoon.

From Peril to Protection: Symbolic Battles

Now Larry and Roxanne's marriage was in jeopardy. Roxanne seriously considered moving back in with her mother. Almost every interaction brought new pain and conflict. If they were to survive as a couple, they would have to find some kind of damage control. They evolved ways of relating that, however painful in themselves, served to contain the even more unbearable feelings of reliving childhood pain or losing the relationship.

One of the first patterns that evolved out of their crisis was that they began to limit their conflicts to symbolic issues. Rather than fight about everything, they developed conflicts around certain things that came to stand for larger issues. They had constant fights over housework, Larry's recreational activities, and their families. This pattern evolved unconsciously, and they were completely unaware of what these things really represented.

These symbolic battles protected them in two ways: they bound up their free floating fears about the future of the relationship into specific areas, leaving other areas, such as supporting each other's careers, relatively free from conflict. By creating conflict over issues that seemed, at least potentially, manageable, they diverted their attention from issues that seemed completely out of control, such as the fear that they'd picked a partner who would never meet their needs.They also concretized their real selves' hopes into specific struggles. Even if they did not win these struggles, all was not lost; their real selves were still engaged.

Let's take the example of housework. As you can imagine, given her perfectionist nature, Roxanne tried to keep a spotless, perfectly organized house, and she expected Larry's help in keeping things that way. Here's one of their typical arguments:

LARRY

I don't know what you're so upset about. I took the towels out of the dryer like you asked, and I put them away.

ROXANNE

If you call cramming them in the linen closet putting them away.

LARRY

What does it matter if every corner is folded perfectly? You're so uptight.

ROXANNE

And you don't care about anything.

LARRY

Look, I told you, if you don't like the way I do things, I've got a perfect solution. I'll pay for someone to come in and help you once a week.

ROXANNE

Oh, that would be great for you. You could go play tennis or go jogging whenever you wanted. But it's more work for me, just getting the house ready for someone to come in and clean it.

Let's look at what this fight symbolized for each of them. As you recall, Roxanne's perfectionism was a desperate attempt to win her mother's admiration and ward off her criticism. She needed Larry to admire her efforts, not resent them. And she needed him to help her keep the order that made her feel safe.

For Larry, the fight about housework symbolized his relationship with his mother. Was he going to have to stay in the house and take care of her, or could he be free of her intrusive neediness and go outside to play? Outwardly, his response to Roxanne was similar to his response to his mother: he pretended to care and be dutiful (he did take the towels out of the dryer). But this marriage also gave him an opportunity to fight against that role as he had never done with his mother, both covertly, by putting the towels back in a way he knew would annoy his wife, and overtly, by criticizing her for being too uptight.

Scripts

Limiting the conflict to certain areas provided a great deal of protection from emotional pain, but there remained the problem of how to control their conflict over these symbolic issues. For the marriage to enter the stable, accommodation phase, they had to develop a pattern of relating that, no matter how painful, would be predictable and would limit the damage they did to each other. I use the term *script* to describe these repetitive patterns.

Larry and Roxanne's script went like this: Roxanne would criticize Larry for something he did, and Larry would try to accommodate her or defend himself, but Roxanne would not be satisfied. So Larry would say, in effect, "You're just impossible," and withdraw, either physically by leaving the house for a while, or emotionally by becoming silent. Roxanne, feeling abandoned, would grow angrier. There would be an angry stalemate for several days. Then the ice would melt a little: Larry would act contrite and dutiful, and Roxanne would withhold her criticism. Until the next time Larry provoked her by doing something he knew would annoy her, or the next time Roxanne got anxious and criticized him. Then the pattern would repeat again.

HOW SCRIPTS WORK

The scripts in a relationship are often mutually reinforcing: when one partner starts to act his part, the other partner will usually respond with hers. Even if they grow tired of this process, each partner is waiting for the other to change, like Alphonse and Gaston saying, "You first," "No, you first." Most of us have had the experience of absence making our heart grow fonder. After a separation, perhaps even only of one day, we eagerly look forward to reconnecting with our mate. But not uncommonly the long anticipated reunion turns out to be disappointing: it doesn't take long before we are back in our script, doing and saying the same kinds of things as always.

How does this happen? Remember the discussion in the last chapter about the system of mutual regulation between a child and his parent? Our earliest experiences are of being exquisitely tuned in to another person's emotional life. Because this regulation is necessary for our survival, we are probably "hard-wired" to unconsciously respond to subtle emotional cues. Certainly our "radar" for responding to cues from our partners is very acute. I've seen couples decode communication and find the tiniest sliver of the content they fear. A husband may come home full of love and enthusiasm, find his wife talking so on the phone, and grow angry and critical. Just one tiny incident—his wife's being on the phone when he wanted to greet her—is enough to bring up abandonment feelings.

A careful exploration of his reaction reveals that it was not that she was on the phone that bothered him, but that she didn't look up and give him the look he associates with her greeting—raising of her eyebrows. This is enough to trigger abandonment feelings. To protect against abandonment, he replaces his warmth and excitement with negative behavior, which cues his wife to act accordingly. So the cycle perpetuates itself.

Scripts become a kind of one-size-fits-all response to any situation. Any time there is stress or conflict, we are likely to go back to our script. Stressful day at the office: better withdraw. Feeling low and lonely: find something in your partner to criticize. Stress, whether from within the relationship—such as the wife talking on the phone when the husband gets home—or from without it—such as a boss's criticism at work—leaves us emotionally vulnerable. We need more tenderness and support from our mates at times like this, but being needy is a source of stress in its own right. We feel anxious that our partner will let us down. Acting out a predictable script makes us feel less anxious.

I know a couple whose script is one of blaming each other. Their car broke down on the Bay Bridge. Rather than call the emergency tow truck, they got into a fight about whose fault it was that they were out of gas. Even though they were still stuck on the bridge, fighting came more easily than trying to decide together on a plan of action. Some scripts actually incorporate a hidden agenda to avoid confronting or even resolving the problem. It is easier to stay in a predictable pattern than to try something new and possibly fail.

Types of Scripts

There are many different scripts in relationships, but they are all based on combinations of fighting or fleeing. Fighting can mean overt conflict, such as yelling or blaming, or covert conflict, such as sabotaging agreements or imposing one's will by sulking. Fleeing can mean physically avoiding each other or just being "tuned out," such as watching television every night.

The four most common scripts that couples enact are:

Anger, which involves both partners in constant crisis and conflict that never gets resolved. Both partners are using their
"fight" defense;
Disengaged, in which both partners flee emotional contact;
Pseudomutual, in which the partners develop a false closeness
that hides their real differences. Both partners are fleeing
real contact by escaping into an imaginary closeness;
Pursuit/avoidance, in which one partner fights for more contact while the other flees from it.

POLARIZATION

In addition to symbolic battles and repetitive scripts, polarization forms an important part of the invisible marriage. It would seem that if two people are opposites on a certain issue there would be loneliness and conflict, but, as with the other aspects of the in-

Table 3–1 Types of Scripts

Script	Defense Partner I	Defense Partner II	Description
Pursuit/Avoidance	Fight	Flight	Pursuit leads to avoidance, which leads to blame and more withdrawal.
Anger	Fight	Fight	Both partners escalate blame and anger, sometimes chronic, other times followed by a brief "honeymoon."
Disengaged	Flight	Flight	Both partners are disengaged, avoid open conflict or intimacy.
Pseudomutual	Flight (fantasy)	Flight (fantasy)	Partners flee real intimacy into fantasy or oneness; conflicts denied or avoided.

visible marriage, the paradox of protection applies here as well. Polarization binds up disappointment, even as it enshrines it in stereotypical roles.

As Larry and Roxanne's relationship moved into the accommodation phase, it became more and more polarized. Larry argued for fun and spontaneity, while Roxanne argued for order and responsibility. Each partner took on one part of a whole self. This polarization sounds like a formula for misery, and to some extent it was. At the invisible marriage level, however, it provided them with protection, allowing each of them to project disowned parts of themselves onto their partner.

Roxanne had had to repress her spontaneous side as a child—she was afraid it would generate her mother's criticism—but of course there was a side to her that wanted to let down and have more fun. By projecting that side onto Larry, she was able to fight against him instead of against herself. Occasionally she could even let herself go along with him.

Larry had a similar internal battle. He spent his childhood being the dutiful son to his mother. Being a good boy made him feel loved and worthwhile. All of his aliveness and all the parts of him that balked at his mother's intrusiveness were invested in sports and outdoor activities. In his polarized relationship with Roxanne, it was as if he gave her the "good boy" part of him to hold, like a coat, while he went outside to play. Just as it had for Roxanne, a painful internal conflict became externalized, allowing Larry to feel that he was reacting to Roxanne rather than feeling his own turmoil.

Here are some other polarizing techniques used by couples: I will be loving/you will be stern; I will be competent/you will be self-effacing; I will handle people/you will handle material things; I will pursue contact/you will pursue solitude; I will express anger/ you will express sadness.

Just as they were for Larry and Roxanne, these tradeoffs are attempts to shore up and protect each other. A man who finds it easier to be angry than sad will find comfort in a relationship in which his partner is the only one who expresses sad feelings. A woman who felt as a child that if she went her own way she would be abandoned will find a secret solace in having a possessive mate— she can use him as an excuse for not risking individuation. It is easier for her to say to herself that "Jack would never let me do that" than to admit to her own fear that no one will love her if she is independent.

TRADITIONAL SEX ROLES

One example of this kind of polarization is the relationship in which the woman agrees to take care of the man's emotional needs and restrain her own assertive impulses, in return for being physically and economically protected. The man, in turn, agrees to let his mate carry the feeling side for both of them in return for his acting strong and stoical. Most couples learned these traditional sex roles as children. Boys were told not to cry and girls were told to be nurturing and not to be aggressive. As children they learned to

be ashamed of the parts of themselves that didn't fit those stereotypes. This shame persists into their adult lives.

Many of the couples I see today have made an overt agreement
to try and change these roles. Men are raising children and learning to express their feelings, while women are working and learning to assert themselves. This represents great progress toward
meeting the needs of their real selves to express wholeness, but
their defensive selves are often not so comfortable with the risks.
The defensive selves would just as soon go on doing the thing they
know best, which is to act out *part* of a person. While overtly seeking equality, many couples continue to have covert expectations
that the man will suppress his emotional neediness and the woman
will suppress her strength. The conflict between their overt efforts
to change these roles and the invisible marriage's effort to preserve
them leaves both sides feeling bewildered. They do not see that
the gender roles offer protection from shame, even as they stymie
growth. Nor do they see that changing them to promote growth
without evoking shame can be a slow process that will require their
mutual effort and support.

TOO CLOSE FOR COMFORT

Love is an expansive feeling. When we are in love we feel that the
whole world is our acre. Such expansion is always followed by a
feeling of disappointment. Despite the efforts of some of the sixties gurus to create a state of permanent bliss, such a rhythm is
part of life. A healthy couple falls in and out of love all the time.
The pattern of emotional expansion and contraction is one of the
things that gets regulated between a mother and a child. When this
regulation has been sufficient, the real self becomes elastic enough
to handle this expansion and contraction; it's part of life.

But if it hasn't been, the defensive self may not be comfortable
with this pattern. If our childhood experience of expansive feelings was like a balloon always getting popped, we learn to keep
ourselves from expanding. The experience of being caught un-
guarded in such an expansive feeling can induce powerful feelings
of shame. To protect ourselves against shame and disappointment

in adult relationships, we are likely to fall back on known and predictable ways of reacting to our partner, such as bickering or avoiding each other. And we are likely to initiate these behaviors at precisely the point we are most vulnerable: when real closeness is possible.

After some time in therapy, Larry and Roxanne were making real progress. They had broken out of their pursuit/avoidance script in several important ways. Larry had planned a ski trip with his brother, and Roxanne had given him her wholehearted support. And Larry had, on his own, arranged for a babysitter and a dinner at a nice restaurant, not, as he put it, "a coupon restaurant that had a deal advertised in the paper."

A week after they reported this progress, they came into my office in a crisis. Larry was planning another ski trip, this one for a full week, and he was going "whether Roxanne liked it or not." Roxanne sat on the couch, looking quietly devastated. Then she composed herself and began her usual round of accusations. "You only care for yourself, you don't know what I'll have to go through getting the kids ready for school by myself." Larry began to withdraw under his counteraccusation that Roxanne was being impossible again. They had taken one step forward and two steps back. Afraid of getting hurt if they risked closeness, they had replaced the intimacy of their restaurant date with the familiarity of their old script.

Regulating closeness is one of the important defensive functions of the invisible marriage. Many relationships have a kind of thermostat that registers the emotional temperature. When the defensive selves feel the partners are getting too close, they kick on the "cooling cycle" of their script. Conversely, if they get too far apart, the defensive selves, fearing abandonment, will initiate a turn toward each other.

BEYOND PROTECTION

We have seen some of the important ways the invisible marriage protects couples from pain: reenactment of childhood scenarios, symbolic battles, repetitive scripts, polarization, regulating closeness. Many psychologists look upon such aspects of relationship as pathological. I disagree. I believe that the protection offered by the invisible marriage provides a starting place for work on the relationship. I sometimes congratulate couples who are locked in an endless battle for not giving up. Underneath the endless complaints of a blaming relationship lie the yearnings of the real self for appreciation and understanding.

In the next section of this book, we will look at some of the most common problems couples have. We will seek to understand the unconscious forces that make these problems so difficult to resolve. We will also be looking at how, albeit in a very roundabout way, our responses to these problems are attempts to communicate something of our deepest fears and our deepest needs to our partner.

II

Visible Problems, Invisible Roots

4

Anger
and
Escalation

◠◡◠

. . . maybe by his curse alone he will attain his object—
that is convince himself that he is a man and not a
piano-key!

DOSTOYEVSKY

A few years ago I led a discussion group for couples with young children. I thought that they would discuss childrearing issues, but the topic they most wanted to discuss was anger and fighting. The group was divided: roughly half thought that fighting and anger between spouses could be productive, the other half thought it was destructive. There was even disagreement between husbands and wives in the same couple. I invited the group to talk about how anger had been handled in their own families.

Again the group was divided. Half the participants reported that their parents never fought or displayed anger in front of them. They complained about getting no sense of the way conflicts get resolved or of their parents' emotional reality. The other half spoke movingly of feeling traumatized by their parents' anger and of constantly worrying whether their families would hold together, or else they were numbed by the endless cycles of bitter conflict. Interestingly, many of the couples were made up of one partner from each camp, as if each were looking to the other for a different experience around anger than they had had in their own families.

Not only are couples divided about whether anger is constructive or destructive, but couples therapists are as well. Some see the healthy expression of anger as essential to relationships while others feel that partners must suppress their anger and develop better communication skills.

One solution to this confusion is to understand the dual nature of anger. On the one hand it can be a kind of communication to your partner, and on the other it can serve merely to preserve or restore your sense of self. Sometimes anger can be clarifying, even liberating, but angry venting can be an excuse to stay stuck.

WHAT IS ANGER?

Think of a little child having a tantrum: the child is trying desperately to communicate his great unhappiness, and he is making a request that the adult rectify the situation. Yet, if we come too close, we are liable to get kicked, so the child's anger is also trying to push us away, to defend himself and assert his need for emotional space. His kicking and flailing is also a way to discharge pent-up frustration. The child's anger is really a complex mixture of biological and emotional expressions.

Freud focused on the biological side of anger, and on the problem of integrating this basic drive into the ego. To a Freudian couples therapist, each partner must come to terms with and learn to sublimate his basic desire to dominate or hurt his spouse.

Heinz Kohut provided a different view of anger. He divided anger into two categories: *mature aggression* and *narcissistic rage*. In mature aggression anger functions as part of the real self. Mature aggression attempts to communicate about an emotional injury or to eliminate an obstacle that prevents us from getting what we want.

Narcissistic rage is something different. When we feel so injured that we are on the verge of falling apart, narcissistic rage takes over and becomes a kind of alternate self. Its only purpose is to preserve some sense of power and cohesion in the face of emotional turmoil. Here are some of Kohut's examples of narcissistic rage: revenge, righting a wrong, undoing a hurt by any means, inflicting on others injuries that we are suffering ourselves, preventive attack, trying to turn a passive position into an active one. They are all characterized by an absence of empathy toward the person we are angry with. That person is momentarily reduced to a thing, a mere object of our anger. For this reason, narcissistic rage is terrifying to be around. It can also be baffling or even terrifying to the person expressing it. We have all had the experience of saying hurtful things that we later regret or can't even imagine having said.

The difference between Kohut's view of anger and Freud's is profound. Freud felt anger was destructive and must be controlled. Kohut believed that anger (or specifically narcissistic rage) made sense when looked at from the point of view of a person desperately trying to defend himself against intolerable feelings. Just as a tantruming child needs to know that he has not severed his emotional ties and can still be loved, so the angry adult needs Kohut's understanding of rage, which implicitly restores empathy. Offering this empathy goes a long way to dissipating the rage.

This is particularly important in relationships. I recently saw a couple where the wife had been enraged at her husband for years. Almost every comment she made to him was cutting and critical. When I was able to trace her anger back to a terrible incident of abandonment that happened early in their relationship (he had broken up with her for a month when they found out she was pregnant) and let her know that I could understand how her anger protected her from feeling vulnerable again to abandonment, she became a different person. Her anger dissipated and she looked at her husband with a new expression, one that was simultaneously tender and wary.

WHY SOME PEOPLE ARE PRONE TO RAGE

Even though angry people can appear powerful, chronic anger masks a very fragile sense of self. If a child succeeds in getting his way through tantruming, it is a hollow victory: bullying his parents into giving in makes a child feel ashamed of himself and emotionally abandoned. An angry, reactive child is operating solely from his defensive self; his real self remains hidden.

Many adults are particularly prone to rage when they don't have their mirroring needs met. A wife turns icily dismissive of her husband when he fails to follow her conversation; a husband says hurtful things about his wife's sexual responsiveness. Such people appear cruel and selfish, but inside they feel like abandoned children, desperately trying to shore up a sense of power in the face of the terrible feeling that they can never make an impact on those they depend on. Their rage at their partner's mirroring failures stems from transference of childhood abandonment, as well as abandonment's cousin, shame.

As we saw in Chapter 2, when a child's desire to have his excited feelings mirrored is met with criticism, shame develops. Anger is a common defense against this shame. The sequence of feeling expansive, feeling rejected or criticized, and responding with anger becomes ingrained. Since falling in love makes us feel expansive, the disappointment that inevitably occurs in relationships can trigger this sequence. For shame- and anger-prone people, the sequence can completely dominate the relationship.

THE SELF-DEFEATING NATURE OF NARCISSISTIC RAGE

Even if narcissistic rage preserves some sense of mastery when a situation feels emotionally out of control, it is inevitably self-defeating. What we really want is to have our disappointments alleviated: to have our partner admire or understand us. But our anger engenders distance and reproach, which only reinforce our underlying feelings of abandonment and shame.

For example, I know a widower who married a woman with three children. He tried desperately to make the situation work and to be a good father to the three needy children. He tried to organize family trips, and he worked hard to set limits for the children. Unfortunately, as often happens to stepparents, his efforts were rebuffed, and the mother and her children formed an alliance to exclude him. The kids resisted his attempts at fathering and accused him of being too heavy. Caught in the middle, the mother sided with her children. Already vulnerable from the death of his first wife, and feeling that his accurate perceptions of what the children needed were being distorted, he reacted with anger. Tragically, this only reinforced the family's perception of him as a bully. His attempts to form a loving family and help the children went out the window, and they eventually divorced. What had begun as an expansive expression of his real self ended in defensive rancor.

Because anger is such a powerful emotion, it tends to take over and force other feelings and even other mental processes out of the picture. We often do not feel the sadness that lies underneath the anger. We sometimes get so wrapped up in anger that we have difficulty thinking clearly. We lose track of what we were originally angry about, and lose our ability to speak clearly or to listen accurately. Both our own experience and our partner's actions end up being distorted.

For couples where one partner's defensive self uses anger and the other uses flight, anger engenders a pursuit/avoidance script. But in couples where both partners are anger-prone, an escalating pattern develops in which attacks trigger counterattacks. Each partner's attempt to communicate is provocative to the other. They are trying, in the words of the Bruce Springsteen song, to put out a fire with gasoline.

ANGER SCRIPTS

We all know couples for whom anger becomes a way of life. Chronically unhappy, these couples battle endlessly, but many stay together for long periods, even for life. Equally surprising, they are as likely to be in love and have real affection for each other as couples who don't fight at all.

These couples may have a dozen fights a month, but they really have only one fight, which they repeat endlessly. They are fighting for survival. They feel that they will not survive being abandoned by their partner, or having their privacy intruded on, or being exposed to shame or ridicule.

The pattern of escalation is very sudden. Each partner is very attuned to messages of blame or shame from the other, and each is ready to respond with a garbage bag full of countercomplaints. A discussion about who should pick up the dry cleaning devolves in an instant into who is more selfish, who is not making enough money, or whose family is the more dysfunctional!

However painful these scripts may seem to the outsider, most couples have learned what they can tolerate. They have mechanisms in place to break off when it gets too hot for comfort: one partner will stomp off, or there will be stony silence for a while. Such scripts bind up disappointment. The wife who yells, "You don't give a damn about me or your family," still feels abandoned, but while she is yelling the pain feels bearable. And she is getting some kind of response from her husband, even if it is not one that meets her underlying need for more contact. In angry relationship scripts, the fight becomes part of a relationship system.

Marriage for these couples resembles the relations between two hostile superpowers: every act can seem charged with threat and tension, and every move toward a sensitive area is met with an immediate counterattack. Like two nuclear powers, there is little room for intermediate actions. All safety is achieved by the threat of "dropping the big one."

Just as two superpowers can find stability in such a world of mutual threats and recrimination, so can a couple who have evolved an anger script. It's an emotional Cold War, but it protects the couple from more destructive conflict. Fighting becomes a substitute for feeling, so that each partner does not have to experience their inner pain around intrusion or abandonment. Fighting becomes a substitute for intimacy, so that each partner does not have to take the risk of being hurt again.

It is important to note that some angry relationships devolve into abusive situations. While the underlying dynamics may be the same, the safety of one or both of the partners is threatened. Such relationships need professional help.

Angry relationships present a paradox. Despite the misery it creates, the anger also carries the emotional life of the relationship. In fighting with each other, both partners are in some way expressing their hope for change. They are at least trying to be strident or loud enough to have an impact. Anger can be the way one partner reveals to another the deep truth about areas where they are wounded. It can be a door that opens onto childhood and shows how we are still carrying wounds from the past.

Because of this complexity, there is no "one-size-fits-all" prescription for handling anger in relationships. Some people need to quit yelling and really listen to each other, and some people need to start yelling to find out the truth about what's really bothering them. Some couples need to stop going around endlessly about their feelings and decide who is going to do the dishes, and some couples need to go deeply into their feelings to get at the core issues that underlie their largely symbolic arguments about something like housework. Many, if not most, couples need to do both: they need to stop battling and start negotiating solutions to daily problems, and they need to carry a battle through to a point where deep, underlying issues are heard and acknowledged.

For all of these couples, learning to distinguish between real and defensive anger is an important first step in changing their script.

REAL ANGER AND DEFENSIVE ANGER

Heinz Kohut's distinction between narcissistic rage and mature anger is very useful. However, rather than being two completely different feelings, they are, in practice, more like two entwined components of the same feeling. Defensive outbursts may seek merely to protect or hurt, but there is an element of the real self's

needs and experiences hidden inside. The key to working success-
fully with anger in relationships is to begin to unravel these two
strands.

Anger that comes from the real self can be a profound expression of our deepest feelings. It is a statement of the fact that we
are not getting our needs met, whether those needs are for more
contact or for more independence. Anger from the real self always
contains a request for change. If the real self feels abandoned, the
anger will contain a message of "Listen to me." If the real self feels
intruded upon, the message will be "Leave me alone."

Defensive anger doesn't carry a request, it carries a warning:
"Back off." Our defensive self, in fact, may say the exact opposite
of what we want. If we are feeling abandoned by our partner, we
may say in anger something like, "Just get out of here, I don't want
to see you at all." Such anger seeks to protect the real self from
getting hurt again.

It is difficult to make the distinction between real and defensive anger, especially in the heat of the moment. However, even
as part of an attempt to make up after a fight, this distinction can
have a tremendous impact on relationship. Let's take a number of
examples to illustrate the difference between real and defensive
anger.

A young woman student and her boyfriend, a young lawyer, are having dinner at a restaurant. The man alludes to
their spending the night together, even though he has
agreed to give the woman more space this week to study
for an important exam. Rather than dealing with the real
issues of her needs for consistency, mirroring of her anxiety about the test, or protection from intrusion, she tries to
regain a sense of power by shaming him: "I thought you had
work to do. Maybe you're just trying to get fired so you can
go on unemployment and play more golf."

A couple has gone to a free concert of a group that used to
be popular in the sixties. The man finds the event very
nostalgic; it reminds him of days when he was young and
free of the responsibilities of career and family. On the way
home his wife punctures his good mood with a long com-

plaint about how she's so busy and he didn't do the chores he'd promised. Instead of trying to defend his good mood from her intrusion or trying to get a mirroring response to his feelings, he counterattacks, telling her how he's sick of her complaining all the time, how she can't even enjoy a concert any more, and how everyone can notice her heavy thighs when she wears shorts.

A couple has been discussing their Thanksgiving guest list. They have agreed not to invite anyone until they can sit down and hammer out the list together, but when Cousin Bob calls, the wife hears her husband invite him. The issue is the way his loyalty to his family makes her feel abandoned, but instead of dealing with that, she threatens to abandon him by being loyal to her own family: "I can't believe you invited Bob. He's a complete jerk. Now you'll have someone to watch the game with. Well, I hope the TV does a good job cooking the turkey, cause I'm having dinner at my mother's."

These defensive responses serve only to shore up the angry partner's shaky sense of self-cohesion; they do nothing to facilitate the real self getting what it needs.

Let's look at one couple's struggle to break their anger script and deal with the real issues underneath.

DAN AND ALISE

Dan, 35, was a freelance journalist and short story writer. His wife, Alise, had just started her own business as a decorator. Here's a typical fight they had. Alise needed to make a bill for her business and she decided to create it on Dan's computer. When he came home he found that she was busily creating her form, feeling very proud of herself. When Dan went to look, however, he saw that, since she really did not know how to use the computer, she was creating her form at the end of the last page of his latest story. She hadn't actually damaged anything he'd written, but Dan was nevertheless enraged.

"I simply went off the deep end," he reported. "I told her to get up, that I would finish the job. When she objected to the way I was doing it, I started to yell at her and call her stupid and half a dozen other names." Alise reacted in kind, and soon they were in a real donnybrook, with each of them digging down into old resentments and hurling them at each other.

DAN

If you're too damned stupid to know how to use this machine, let me do it.

ALISE

I'm doing fine! I don't need help from some male god.

DAN

Oh, screw you and your male god stuff. I'm trying to help you get this done right.

ALISE

Help? You're the most selfish man on earth. You've got to control everything. What's really bugging you is that I might be able to do this myself, that I might not need you. You just want a woman to say "pretty please" and "my hero" to you!

DAN

That's it! That's the last straw! You're the most hate-filled harpy that's ever been born. You're out to destroy anyone who comes near you. Get out of my study, and while you're at it, why don't you get out of my life!

ALISE

With pleasure.

This was fairly typical of their script. Dan would often try to be the nice guy in the relationship and act like he was sincerely trying to support Alise in her life, but inevitably something would trigger his rage and he would attack. To Alise, these attacks seemed to come out of the blue. When that happened, Alise would respond by going to war. She would try to throw anything she could at Dan. So the fighting would escalate, often until they were on the brink of breaking up. But they never did break up. When they would get to the brink, they would move to reconcile—until the next fight. In order to break this cycle, each of them had to begin looking at themselves, instead of blaming each other.

Dan

I sensed that Dan felt regret about some of the things he'd said to Alise, so I decided to start with him. I asked if he was willing to step back from his fight with Alise for a little while and look at his own issues, and he agreed. Dan realized how violated he felt about his wife's using his computer, and how much he'd been afraid to express any limits or discomfort with it. "I'm always trying to be nice. I like to share things. But I guess I also need my privacy, and I'm reluctant to tell Alise what I need. I'm afraid she'll think I'm selfish, or that I put my career ahead of hers. So instead I just sit on it, and then end up blowing up. The thing that really hurts is that she just sees me as a jerk because I blew up at her, and now it will be twice as sensitive a subject to bring up and resolve."

I wondered with Dan why he seemed to have no idea how to set a limit for himself against intrusion. This led to a discussion of his family of origin. Dan was the oldest son in a large, angry family. "Sometimes I think the only thing my parents agreed on was that they both liked me," he told me. His parents would often turn to him to solve their disputes. Other times they would both lavish praise on him, out of proportion to his real merits. Dan never had a sense of privacy. "My whole life belonged to my parents. They would rage around, and I carried all the responsibility." Despite the praise, Dan never felt respected as a person in his own right. He was always meeting his parents' needs for an idealizable selfobject. Although being an idealizable hero got him his parents' admiration, it never felt like they saw or respected his real self. Dan had a lot of suppressed rage about this, and a tremendous need to set limits and have some separateness.

But in his relationship with Alise, he kept alternating between trying to be the idealizable good guy and blowing up in fits of defensive anger. Though the anger carried his yearning to finally have his separateness respected, the yearning was hidden behind criticism of Alise. Because this just started a chain reaction of anger that never got resolved, he never got closer to getting the privacy his real self vitally needed. At no time in his childhood had anyone told him that he had such a right. Without an intrinsic sense that he could have his own computer and not share it, he could only attack Alise to shore up some sense of control against an intolerable loss of self.

When Dan was fighting with Alise, he was also fighting with the ghosts of his mother and father. That was too big a fight to ever win. I told Dan to imagine that his mother and father were in the room with us, sitting in the empty chairs across from him. I asked him to tell each of his parents in turn what his needs were about the computer. After a moment, he began. "It's my computer. It's all mine. It's where I do my work. I don't want you coming in to my study. I don't want you touching it. I don't want you telling me what to write, or how to live my life." Dan looked like he was struggling to hold back tears. He reminded me of a 15-year-old boy. I let him compose himself for a few minutes and come back to the present. "Would you like to tell Alise the same thing?" He hesitated a minute, as if anticipating that it would just start up the same fight again. But when he turned from the empty chairs to face his wife, he saw that her face was greatly softened.

"Will you promise never to use my computer without my permission?"

"Yes," Alise answered softly.

"No exceptions?"

"No exceptions," Alise replied, smiling. This may seem like a small step, but it was the first time in years that they had been able to agree on anything.

Alise

Alise's father, who had been a semipro baseball player, had always wanted a son to fulfill his unmet dreams of athletic success. Alise was the youngest of three daughters. "He tried to make me into his son, but I wasn't a natural athlete, so instead he just used to ridicule me." As a teenager, Alise had learned how to handle her father's ridicule. She either ignored him or was very sarcastic. This worked—for the most part, her father backed off. Alise grew up to become fiercely independent and highly competitive. She was determined that no one would catch her being vulnerable, that no one would see her as she was as a child, on the ballfield with her father, awkwardly trying to learn how to throw and catch. But underneath she was still a hurt little girl who was deeply ashamed of disappointing her father. She hid this hurt under a sharp tongue and a streetfighter's instinct for combat.

In Dan, she had found someone to keep sparring with. Dan's critical outbursts were familiar territory. She knew how to keep him at bay and intimidated—just as she had done as a teenager to her father. Her choice of mate allowed her to use familiar defenses, but it did nothing to help her get what she really wanted: a partner who would accept her for who she was, rather than one to whom she had to constantly prove herself.

Sometimes the only way to get beyond anger is to go through it. Just getting in touch with the issue of her father's criticism didn't make it go away, and it didn't make her any less angry at Dan for his criticism. Instead of cooling down their conflict, Alise needed to carry it through to a different conclusion. She needed to stay in the fight long enough until she had discharged her stored-up anger.

I suggested that Alise might need some time to tell Dan how angry she was, without being interrupted. Dan agreed that he would just listen to whatever Alise had to say for fifteen minutes.

It took a little while for Alise to warm up, but after she got going she filled her time with expressions of her pent-up anger: "You're just a bully, Dan. I can't stand it when you call me stupid. You act so nice one minute, then you turn abusive. Go yell at your mother if she's the one you're angry at, but just leave me out of it! You've got to stop. I won't take it anymore. I just can't take it anymore!"

Alise had been yelling for most of her fifteen minutes. Now she sat and tried to catch her breath. Dan was sitting across from her. He was agitated; he was dying to reply and defend himself, but he'd held his tongue and kept his part of the bargain.

Like the agreement about the computer, this interaction was a small success for a couple that had had few successful interactions. Alise had managed to stay with her anger and get to the root—her need to protect herself from Dan's attacks—and Dan had managed to hear her rather than counterattack. This time Alise's anger, rather than being a destructive force, had actually been a way for them to break out of their script.

MOVING BEYOND ANGER

There are no panaceas for curing angry relationships, but there are some things you can do, both independently and as a couple, to try to resolve some of the hostility. The first step involves making a commitment to change. A good place to start is to agree that there is too much anger and hurt in the relationship, and that, without assigning blame, you'd both like things to improve. Falling into the old script here is very possible, since just acknowledging your hope for change makes you vulnerable. It's best to have the discussion when things are peaceful, rather than in the middle of a fight. The main aim at this point is simply to express your preference and willingness to make things better.

The second and most important step is taking responsibility for your own anger. Relationships are a system, and the only part of that system you can directly change is your own. This does not mean replacing blame for your partner with blaming yourself. What it does mean is taking a look at the way your angry script is keeping you from getting what you need from your relationship. To do this, you need not to turn your anger off, but to take it more seriously. Learning to distinguish between real and defensive anger is at the heart of this.

LISTENING TO YOUR OWN ANGER

Most of the time couples who are involved in an anger script are so busy attacking that they don't hear where the other person is coming from. It would be easy to say that such people are so convinced that they're right that they don't care to listen to the other side of things. However, as Heinz Kohut realized, they are not so much trying to convince their partner of the rightness of their position as they are trying to protect a fragile part of their own self from further injury.

The reason that Dan and Alise were not able to speak of their real feelings and attacked each other instead is that they didn't believe that their feelings were valid. Despite his outrage, Dan didn't really believe that people have a right to be angry when their privacy is invaded, and Alise, for all her bluster, didn't really believe that she had a right to a relationship that was free of emotional abuse. Their anger merely covered their lack of certainty.

One way to begin to reclaim real anger from defensive anger is to realize that there is no such thing as an invalid feeling. A feeling may not accurately correspond to the logical reality of the present situation, but that is because feelings come from a different area of reality than logic. Feelings, like the unconscious, do not conform to our usual sense of time. Alise may not have had the slightest intention to invade Dan's space when she used his computer, but to Dan, at that moment, she was just like his mother, who never respected his separateness. Dan's anger and criticism of Alise may have been entirely a product of the moment, but for Alise it carried the exact same message as her father's chronic disappointment in her. These feelings should not be discounted. When they are, communication suffers.

Both Dan and Alise's positions were valid. The problem with their relationship wasn't that they fought too much, but that they didn't take the positions they were fighting from seriously enough to fight for them in a productive way. Each wanted to be heard and respected by the other, but the first step was hearing and respecting themselves. Listening to their own anger helped remove the need for a protective script, and opened the way for a more truly intimate relationship.

As we learned in Chapter 2, most threats to the self come from feelings of being abandoned, intruded upon, or made to feel ashamed. As a child you had no alternative to the defensive reactions of fight or flight. Now, as an adult, you can work with those feelings. Try saying the following to yourself: "My spouse's actions have made me feel abandoned or intruded on or ashamed of myself. These were feelings I had as a child. Now, as an adult, I realize that I have an absolute right to protect myself from these feelings by telling my partner what I need and what my limits are about his or her behavior."

Of course these feelings will still come up in any relationship. No partner is perfect, and conflicts will arise. Something you want will make your partner feel abandoned. Something your partner says that seems to them just a statement of fact will make you feel criticized and ashamed. If you feel entitled to your anger when these things happen, you will be better able to express it in a way that can be heard, and better able to find solutions to the problem. Believing in the validity of your own anger is a step toward being able both to express your needs clearly and to listen more effectively to your partner's feelings. Paradoxically, if you know that your anger is carrying some portion of rightness or truth, you are less prone to try and prove yourself right and your partner wrong. A good fight then becomes an opportunity to clear the air and learn something about yourself and your partner. Anger becomes a bridge toward intimacy, rather than a brick in a protective wall.

Pursuit
and Avoidance

5

Why, love, does it
make such a difference
not to be heard
in spite of self

or what we may feel
one for the other
but as a hammer
to drive again

bent nail
into old hurt?

ROBERT CREELEY

Marriages in which one partner pursues emotional contact and the other tries desperately to avoid it are so common that we may come to see them as part of the human condition, rather than as part of the invisible marriage. Indeed, some recent books ascribe this pattern to intrinsic differences between the sexes, who apparently come from different planets. Though in our culture it is usually the woman who pursues and the man who withdraws, there are many couples where the man pursues contact from an emotionally unavailable woman. Whoever plays the roles of pursuer and pursued, what is really happening is that both partners are unconsciously cooperating to avoid intimacy rather than create it.

Occasionally, the pursuit and avoidance will lead to a fight, and this will come to substitute for real contact, but more often the conflict will only freeze the partners further in their roles, and the script will repeat again. The men will stereotype their wives as angry, and rationalize their emotional withdrawal, and the women will stereotype the men as impossible and incapable of loving or showing emotion.

The fact that women often feel emotionally deprived in marriage has been well documented. But how much happier are the men, locked in their emotional refuges of work and television or drugs and alcohol? Many men are truly bewildered. They replicate their fathers' behavior as good breadwinners, who see to it that things run smoothly, and still they find themselves beset with criticism from their angry wives, who demand that they open up and express what's going on inside them. Some don't understand what their wives really want; they experience themselves as emotionally straightforward, without any deep emotional secrets. Others are very out of touch with their emotions, and couldn't open up even if they wanted to. Still others fear that if they open up their partners will pounce on them. What these men are hearing is something like, "Open up and be vulnerable, you emotionally incompetent jerk."

As with other aspects of the invisible marriage, however, there is more to this picture of angry women and impossible men than meets the eye. Rather than fighting some archetypal battle of the sexes, both the pursuer and the pursued are unconsciously choosing conflict over intimacy. As in other scripts, the pursuit and avoidance script is an amalgam of real self needs and defensive self protections.

MERGERS AND DISTANCERS

We all know people who seek intimacy and closeness, and others who are happier being more independent and spending time alone. One woman I know relishes her vacations in a lakeside cabin with three cousins, their wives, and their children. They eat big meals, sing songs all night, and share in activities like fishing and hiking. There is very little privacy or solitude. She is married to a man who loves to go on solitary walks and who spent several vacations in his bachelor years hiking alone in Nepal. This man does not accompany his wife to the lakeside cabin, but uses the vacation to luxuriate in the emptiness of their home while his wife is away.

How we choose to spend our vacations is a matter of taste or even style. It reflects our preferences, but is hardly a matter of survival. For many people, however, issues of closeness or distance aren't questions of preference. The need to seek connection with others or the need to avoid feeling controlled or invaded by others are paramount. They reflect the fact that, as children, these people were emotionally abandoned in some painful way, or else their parents did not sufficiently respect and foster their individuality.

I will use the term *mergers* for those who seek connection above all else. For mergers, the absence of someone who understands and acknowledges them feels like a threat to their very lives. They need to feel seen to feel alive. *Distancers* are the mirror opposite: for them the idea of being perfectly at one with another person feels like death by suffocation. Distancers fear that if someone sees inside them they will be able to take over and control them. Avoiding being seen becomes an emotional necessity.

When two mergers form a relationship, the result is liable to be either a flight to oneness of the pseudomutual script, or a script of anger as they both try to be the one that gets seen. When two distancers get together, they will create a disengaged relationship.

A distancer and a merger will evolve a pursuit/avoidance script. Before we look at this script in detail, let's look at the unconscious dynamics of each partner.

Mergers

People who pursue connection above all else are usually responding to the fact that they were once emotionally abandoned. As a result of this early abandonment, they are flooded with unmet needs and long for a mirroring response from their mates to their every feeling. This is a set-up for disappointment, and this disappointment reinforces the belief that they will always be abandoned and that their needs themselves are illegitimate. Rather than see these underlying feelings, all their mates are likely to see is their relentless pursuit of contact and their criticism. The underlying feelings of hopelessness and worthlessness remain hidden.

To deal with their chronic disappointment, they rely on their defensive self and its fight or flight responses. They either substitute a fight for intimacy or flee into romantic fantasy. Long ago they learned that kicking up a fuss would at least get some attention, and that they would not feel the pain of their abandonment in the midst of emotional drama. And long ago they developed the consoling fantasy of someday meeting someone who would take away their feelings of emptiness.

Unfortunately, these strategies do not work well in adult relationships. Desperately fighting with our partners to keep them from abandoning us just drives them further away. And no real person can match the compensatory fantasy. Even in the moments when mergers do feel understood, they do not feel fulfilled, because they end up focusing on their fear that the connection will go away. The pursuit takes the place of intimacy, and the drama of the pursuit hides the underlying feelings of abandonment.

Distancers

Distancers fear that if someone gets too close to them they will be taken advantage of or humiliated. They are not hermits who loathe contact. On the contrary, underneath their distancing defenses they are often very needy. They do not want anyone to see their neediness because they fear that it is an invitation to be intruded on. In early childhood they were called upon to mirror their parents or to be idealizable, rather than being mirrored themselves.

In order to cope with these painful experiences, distancers made a decision not to let others see what they were feeling. Since emotions are by their very nature spontaneous, distancers learned to suppress their spontaneity. To do this they had to move their aliveness out of their hearts and bodies—where feelings live—and into their minds, where they could substitute thinking for feeling. Thoughts are less spontaneous than feelings. Our language itself reflects this: we speak of feeling directly ("I was feeling sad") but we speak of thinking *about* something. This is why distancers have such a hard time expressing their feelings—they can tell you what they think *about* the situation, but they have by long habit distanced themselves from experiencing how it affects them directly. Having opinions or judgments is much safer than having needs or feelings.

Distancers may seek to be admired from afar, thus repeating their childhood pattern of being idealizable for their parents. Intimacy requires being open to our partner "warts and all," while the person seeking to be admired wants to hide all imperfections. Because they need to remain idealizable, distancers are terrified of failure. They would actually like to be more open and involved with their partners or families, but they fear being rejected or criticized. Their partner's criticism of their lack of availability confirm their worst fears. When they are cornered they will try to argue or prove themselves right. This arguing is very frustrating to the merger, who is seeking contact with her partner's feelings, but it is a survival strategy to the distancer, who fears having his imperfections exposed.

In the same way as mergers replace intimacy with emotional drama, distancers replace it with a power struggle. Because distancers fear criticism, they will often use a passive-aggressive style of outward compliance and hidden resistance. They may try and look like good husbands, but be emotionally unavailable. At the same time, while not overtly seeking contact, distancers do subtle things that covertly call attention to themselves. For example, a husband says he'll pick up the cleaning but then forgets; a wife says she'll be ready by 6:00 but hasn't started dressing by 6:15. This allows distancers to get some of their mirroring needs met—at least they get a *response* from their spouse, while still not exposing any neediness. By subtly making their partner angry, they also have an excuse to remain distant.

Just as underneath their relentless pursuit mergers don't really feel entitled to contact, so underneath their stiff-armed avoidance distancers don't feel really entitled to privacy. Such straightforward statements as, "I don't want to tell you what I'm feeling right now," or even, "I don't want to see you tonight," are very difficult for them.

Both mergers and distancers actually create the response they fear in their partner. By refusing to commit to any plan or sabotaging the agreements they do make, the distancer heightens his partner's anxiety, making her more relentless in her pursuit, while the merger's shrillness drives her partner further away. It is hard for mergers to risk asking for closeness directly, but a simple statement of a request, such as, "Let's get a babysitter on Saturday night" is often much more powerful than "You never pay any attention to me anymore." The former carries the expectation that the merger's needs for contact will be met; the latter carries the burden of her hopelessness.

Rather than taking such risks and asking for what they want, what often happens is that a merger and a distancer will pair up and create a relationship that enables them to keep using their life-long defensive styles.

THE PURSUIT/AVOIDANCE SCRIPT

All too often, the stereotype of the needy woman and the distant man runs true. The wife will be feeling isolated and lonely and will try and initiate some contact. The husband will be lost in his own world of work or television, and will grunt some reply. The frustrated wife will escalate by coming at her husband with a list of complaints, often complaints that have nothing to do with the central issue—her emotional isolation. "Why don't you go mow the lawn, why don't you pick up after yourself?" she'll complain. The husband will still try to put her off. "I'll do it in an hour, okay?" But the wife, now desperate for some kind of a reaction, will keep after him. She may know some button that will surely provoke him, such as, "I bet you'd mow the lawn if it was your mother who was asking." This gets the predictable response—the husband rouses from his distance to counterattack. They will have a brief, angry fight—which is the closest they come in the cycle to any real emotional contact—and then one of them, usually the husband, will stomp off, feeling newly justified in distancing from his angry wife. At some point, things will calm down, and there will be a brief lull before the cycle repeats.

It would seem that this script would be very easy to change. The merger needs to back off and the distancer needs to open up. They could resolve their struggle through compromise. In practice this is quite difficult to achieve. Over and over again I have seen such conflicts move toward resolution, only to have one or another partner sabotage it and reestablish the old pattern. The wife who has demanded that her husband open up will discount his newly expressed feelings by saying, "That's not true, that's not what you really feel." And when a wife lightens up on her demands and becomes more independent, I have often seen the man begin to criticize her new friends or activities.

Couples will even switch roles when their pursuit/avoidance script begins to change. One patient of mine was always demanding that her husband do more of the activities she liked with her, such as attending lectures or concerts, or going to museums. Her husband was a self-described couch potato. They had a low-level conflict about this for years. I told her that her husband seemed content the way he was and would probably not change. I suggested that, if she wanted to go to cultural activities, perhaps she could find other friends to go with her. She did just that; she became a docent at the local museum and soon developed a group of her own friends who enjoyed museums and concerts. After a few weeks her husband grew absolutely furious. He complained that she was never home, that he never got to talk to her any more!

These couples aren't being perverse or hypocritical. Their long-standing conflicts reflect the defensive nature of the script. The pursuit/avoidance script represents a compromise between hope and fear. While mergers seek to compensate for past feelings of abandonment by pursuing contact, they also fear having those long-buried injuries reexposed. They don't really want to completely lose themselves in another. That kind of closeness might uncover a fear, which their neediness keeps hidden, of being intruded on.

Distancers, who fight to keep from feeling intruded upon, don't really want to win the fight. If they were left completely alone, they would become vulnerable to feelings of abandonment. The hidden conflict reflects this pattern of protection. The struggle is a safer alternative to sticking their neck out and asking for the safety and contact that they need.

A first step in changing the pursuit/avoidance script is to lighten the tension of a relationship that can seem like a deadly struggle. I sometimes tell partners that they are each fighting for something very necessary, that one is Minister of Closeness and the other is Minister of Separateness. The Minister of Closeness has the responsibility for seeing that the couple doesn't just drift apart, and the Minister of Separateness has the equally important responsibility of seeing that the two partners don't lose their identities and become a shapeless blob of "we." Humor can help couples understand that what looks like a conflict between enemies is really an unconscious cooperative pattern of protection.

NEEDY MEN AND DISTANCING WOMEN

There are a great many relationships where the pursuit/avoidance works counter to the stereotype—the women avoid the advances of their demanding or angry husbands. Men's emotional neediness often feels to women like a request for mothering. Men also have unconscious memories of feeling perfectly mirrored by their mothers, and will try to recreate these experiences. They assume that their wife will want to hug them whenever they want physical contact. They will expect her to understand what they are feeling without their having to explain themselves. Or they will expect their partners to mirror them by being endlessly interested in what went on at the office, just as their mothers were interested in what went on that day in school. Since these needs are largely unconscious, men don't ask directly for this kind of attention; they just act like they expect it. And if this "mother transference" were pointed out to them, they would probably feel deeply ashamed.

Women often don't want the job of being a kind of mother surrogate to their men, and find such demands an intrusion on their independence. However, because women in our society are conditioned to be warm and nurturing, many women feel obligated to fulfill this role for their partners. A pursuit/avoidance script in which the woman is the distancer helps resolve this contradiction. She can appear to be fulfilling her obligation to be the dutiful wife, while at the same time covertly resisting it by being critical, inattentive, or preoccupied with her own problems. For example, when her husband comes home upset about something that happened at work, she might minimize it, saying, "Don't worry, honey, it will all blow over." Of course, the husband wants her to worry, he is looking for a mirroring experience that will confirm that she knows what he is feeling. Frustrated in his desire for understanding and fearing abandonment, he moves to the next step in their pursuit/avoidance script and starts to criticize her. "You don't know anything about how these things work," he replies. "A corporation's not like some PTA meeting." Then she uses her partner's growing impatience or anger as justification for withdrawing further. "Look, if you're going to be like that, I'm not going to listen. I've got a million things to do around here."

Regardless of who pursues and who avoids intimacy, the result is a script of much unhappiness for both partners. The distancer will always feel intruded upon, and the merger will always feel abandoned.

When you are in such a script, it is very difficult to see the part you play in keeping it going. You are so much more aware of the pain your partner is causing you. It is even more difficult to see that there might be some very good reasons for you to want to keep it going. Yet it is usually the case that both partners have a hidden investment in their pursuit and avoidance script: they are invested in the protection it provides. Overtly the couple is saying, "Don't abandon me"/"Don't control me," but, by pursuing their script, which triggers the very behaviors they are overtly protesting, they are saying, in effect, "Do abandon me" (by being distant and impossible when I pursue you)/"Do control me" (by being critical and demanding when I avoid you). Each partner is then able to keep struggling with these childhood issues of abandonment and intrusion. To understand how this can be, let's look at one couple for whom pursuit and avoidance was safer than real intimacy.

LEE AND WENDY

Lee and Wendy were an attractive, affluent, and very unhappy couple when they came to see me for marital therapy. Wendy had red hair and patrician good looks, while Lee, of Hispanic ancestry, was darkly handsome. Wendy complained that she felt completely unappreciated. "Lee never notices anything I do, never says I look nice. Last week, I made him a special dinner, something I'd been planning for weeks, and he barely mentioned it. I feel that I could be replaced by a robot and he wouldn't notice!" Lee sat in my office with a cold, withdrawn look in his eyes as he listened to Wendy list her complaints about him. But when I asked him how he saw things, his tone was very different than what I expected. He spoke in careful, measured sentences. "I probably should show Wendy more appreciation. I guess I'm just not very good at giving compliments. It's easier to notice her faults." Despite his angry and self-protective expression, his words were saying, "You're right; I agree with you that I'm at fault."

Wendy's anger did not seem particularly allayed by Lee's response, and no wonder—she was after him to show some emotion, and his words were flat and devoid of feeling. His body language conveyed the truer message, "I'm not going to let you come close to me."

The incident that finally convinced them to seek some counseling involved their son, Peter. Here's how Wendy described it: "Last week our son's hamster died. He came running into our room absolutely distraught. He needed his father. But where was Lee? Watching the game. We ran into the living room and I yelled, 'Turn that thing off and talk to your son. Can't you see he's crying?' He looked at Peter, then looked up and said, 'Haven't you been cleaning the cage?' I lashed back at him, 'Maybe if you were around more things would stay more together.' There we were, arguing about who was at fault, while our little boy was sobbing about his hamster."

The hamster incident became one more pretext for Lee and Wendy to run their script. Their son's grief reminded Wendy of her own feelings that Lee was abandoning her. She dealt with this abandonment by blaming him. Lee felt that Wendy was trying to dictate to him how to feel, and, in classic distancer fashion, he responded to this intrusion with a cold criticism of her actions.

But their son's grief also allowed them to look at their relationship in a different light. They both loved Peter, and both felt bad that, instead of responding to his pain, they had gotten sidetracked into their same old tired conflict. Why couldn't they stop playing their roles of merger and distancer long enough to parent their son together? It turned out that for both Wendy and Lee, those roles were more than the product of longtime habits or of sex-role conditioning. For both of them, they were defensive strategies they'd learned as young children.

Wendy

Wendy came from a successful, professional family. I asked Wendy if her parents often criticized her or were stingy with appreciation, and she replied that it was just the opposite. Her mother, especially, was always proud of her achievements. There was something a little pat about her answer that alerted me. As we talked a little more I began to suspect that, contrary to this consciously held belief about her mother, the memories she was unconsciously carrying with her from childhood were very different.

I asked her what it felt like to have her mother be proud of her, and whether it made her feel secure and important. She answered, "I guess I never thought about that. [long pause] You know, I never really knew if I could trust my mother's bubbliness. I never knew if she really thought I was special, or if I was just like all the friends with whom she kept up such lively conversation. One minute she would be excited over my achievements; the next minute I would be really proud of something and she would just be too busy to notice."

Wendy began to see that her mother, rather than mirroring her childhood excitement, was too wrapped up in her own world to notice. This realization for Wendy crystallized around a particular memory that she had long ago repressed. Wendy studied piano all through her childhood. Sometimes, whether she felt like it or not, her mother would make her play piano for her guests. Regardless of how she herself felt she did, her mother would publicly praise her highly. Now Wendy recalled a painful memory of the other side of the coin. "I had been struggling very hard with a Beethoven sonata. My teacher had been very critical. One day she had me play it through from the beginning without interrupting me, and when I was through she told me I was so good that she wanted me to play the whole piece at a recital. Other students would only be playing shorter pieces or excerpts. I was so thrilled I ran all the way home and burst in to where my mother was talking to some friends. I can still feel her withering look that said 'Don't bother me now.' I just wanted to die."

Wendy felt abandoned by her mother at times like these, and she also felt ashamed. As we saw in Chapter 2, the piano incident is a classic scenario for creating shame. Wendy was excited and expansive and was surprised by her mother's withering disapproval. This memory symbolized many similar incidents.

For Wendy, her mother's praise became a dangerous thing. If she let herself count on it, she was vulnerable to being surprised again. Instead, as children often do, she let her defensive self take over to protect her. She developed a habit of being highly critical. She became the kind of kid who always acts like she knows the right answers, and is scornful of others. Underneath that critical attitude she was actually also very self-critical.

It would seem that, as an adult, Wendy would want to have a kind of "compensation clause" in her marriage contract: "Please give me dependable, consistent recognition for the things I do for you." But this is exactly the opposite of the type of relationship she had with Lee.

Why would Wendy choose an emotionally unavailable man? We can best understand this question by imagining the opposite. Wendy's defensive self survived her mother's inconsistency by learning not to count on people. If Lee were to be present emotionally, all her unmet needs would rush to the surface, flooding her with memories of disappointment and shame. She would be that little girl again, bursting into her mother's living room. And her defensive strategy was to never let that happen again.

So Wendy developed a script with Lee of pursuing him and complaining about his lack of emotion, which had the effect of keeping him shut down. Her defensive self was saying to him, "Please be distant and critical and don't praise me very much. This will keep me from being vulnerable to the terrible feelings of shame I felt for wanting more praise as a child. Also, it will let me project my childhood anger and disappointment onto you, Lee, so I do not have to remember what happened with my mother." In choosing Lee, she had chosen a distancer who would easily fulfill his part in her defensive script.

Lee

Underneath Lee's cold, self-critical demeanor was a lot of unacknowledged anger. It took a long time for him to admit to this anger, much less look for its sources within his marriage and in his family of origin. I approached the issue intellectually, telling him that most people didn't just grow up to want emotional distance, and that I was sure we could find reasons for the way he acted. This allowed enough safety for us to warily proceed to talk about his childhood.

Lee's family was working class, and this was a source of disappointment for his mother, who always considered herself born to better things. Lee's father was a traveling salesman and was gone a great deal of the time. To compensate, Lee's mother turned her attention to him. He was a good student, and his mother would praise his scholastic achievements highly. When I asked Lee what it was like when his mother praised his schoolwork, he replied, "It wasn't really very comfortable. I thought there were strings attached, that I had to make her happy."

Lee's achievements, which represented his moves toward independence, were never enjoyed for their own sake. When his mother praised him, Lee heard a message that went, "Now you're satisfying me. I've been so disappointed in your father, at least now I have someone to be proud of." This was very intrusive, as if his mother were saying that everything Lee did belonged to her. His mother's intrusion also brought up a lot of feelings of shame for him: the more his mother praised him, the more he felt inside that it wasn't deserved, that he could never live up to her expectations.

Lee couldn't express his anger at his mother openly. Instead he learned to wage a low-level battle of noncompliance. He learned to act politely, but underneath this demeanor he was often sullen. He acted indifferent about his own successes. In his senior year of high school, he got a C average, and ended up going to a community college rather than the university his mother had hoped he would attend. In response to his mother's intrusiveness, Lee had taught himself to shut off his own excitement about life. No wonder Wendy complained that, when she tried to make contact, no one was home!

Resistance

Making the link between childhood scenarios and adult relationships is usually not enough to bring about change. It can help couples to be more accepting, but, even armed with self-knowledge and the best of intentions, couples fall back into old scripts again and again. When Lee and Wendy tried to change, they often ended up blaming each other for not doing better, and then fell back into their script, with Wendy being angry and Lee taking responsibility for the problem and then withdrawing into sullen silence. They would even use things they learned in therapy against each other. Wendy would say to Lee, "Look, I'm not your mother, I don't need to live through you, so don't give me that silent treatment. Save it for her the next time she calls." A little knowledge for them was a dangerous thing.

I began to see that, more than anything, Wendy and Lee needed permission to not change, to maintain the safety they had created with their script. As the incident with Peter's hamster showed, they already felt bad about themselves for their relationship. Trying harder to change would just make them feel worse. I said to them, "You two have created a script that works for you, and I think it is very important right now, when so much is coming up from your childhoods, that you not feel like you're failing when you keep acting it out."

One day, Lee took off from work to attend one of Peter's Little League games, but a combination of traffic and last-minute business made him late. Wendy's cold reception was enough to trigger his withdrawal. As it turned out, Wendy had a headache, and was not feeling critical at all. However, when Lee, reacting to what he took as a cue, went into his role of sullen withdrawal, Wendy went into hers, saying, "Once a year you come to his game, and you can't even show some enthusiasm." It is important that couples not feel like failures over incidents like this.

ACCEPTING DEFENSIVE BEHAVIOR

Change happens much more easily in an atmosphere of understanding and acceptance than it does in an atmosphere filled with blame and a sense of failure. You can start by applying this principle to yourself. Instead of focusing on what you do wrong, you can try to understand and accept your defensive behaviors. If you are frequently angry, you can recognize that you must really need the defensive protection of anger right now. If you are trying to create as much distance as possible between your mate and yourself, you can acknowledge the need for the protection from abandonment or intrusion that that distance is providing. You might think that this is a formula to rationalize away your failures, but most often this is not the case. Giving yourself permission to be angry or distant can actually relax your relentless defenses. After all, they are right here, ready to use if you need them.

ASKING FOR CONTACT IN A WAY THAT CAN BE HEARD

Wendy eventually became aware enough of her part in the pursuit and avoidance script that she felt that she had a choice. "Sometimes, I can almost feel the balance point, the moment of decision. I'll be really upset about something with Lee, and I'll walk in, and I can feel that I'm either going to let him have it or I'm going to try and get him to hear me. Some days I'm so irritated, or so hopeless about our relationship, that I'll just go ahead and yell. But other times, I can take a deep breath, approach him slowly, and get him to listen."

Wendy had learned that the way she communicated her feelings often sabotaged her chances of being heard and served to keep the script going, and that, if she allowed herself to take the risk of trying to be heard, Lee would actually be available to hear her. The key was finding a way to say to Lee, "I'm not telling you you're a terrible person, and I'm not trying to control you, I'm just trying to make some contact." This was very vulnerable territory. She feared she would be ignored just as she had been when she burst in on her mother with news of her piano recital. But the times she let herself try and found that Lee was receptive were very important. They were planks on which she could build a new reality about relationships, one that didn't just repeat her childhood experiences.

ASKING FOR PRIVACY

Even though Wendy accused Lee of being selfish, his problem was that he was not selfish enough. As a child he did not feel entitled to his own life, separate from his mother's expectations, and in his relationship with Wendy, he did not really feel entitled to his own interests, his own thoughts and feelings. Ironically, his actions made him look very selfish. He was fighting a defensive battle against intrusion all the time. Underneath his combativeness, he felt helpless to protect himself from a woman's intrusion. He feared that if he gave in to Wendy once, he would forever give up his right to remain separate. The stubborn way that he ignored Wendy's demands was a product not of his selfishness but of his insecurity.

Of course his sullen, passive-aggressive style of resisting Wendy's desire for contact only enraged her and made her look that much more like the controlling woman he feared. It was a self-fulfilling prophecy.

Eventually Lee was also able to learn some new communication skills. In one session, I had Lee spell out to Wendy his plans for watching football the next weekend. At first he was provocative: "I'll watch two college games on Saturday, two pro games on Sunday, and then of course, there's Monday Night Football. I'll talk to you on Sunday night." This, of course, was an invitation to Wendy to start their script. He would be impossible, and she would be angry. But then he stopped himself, and decided to try. "I was just kidding. The really important game to me is the '49ers on Sunday. I don't care that much about the college games. If you'll agree not to interrupt me on Sunday morning, I'll spend Saturday with you and Peter, and we can do whatever you want." Maintaining a separate life, including separate interests, separate friends, even separate opinions, thoughts, and feelings, is a vital part of being in a relationship. Mergers will often mistake this separateness for abandonment and try to stop it. But the way that distancers try to achieve it is also part of the problem. Distancers need to be able to say to their merger partners, "This is the amount of privacy I need, and this is how much I'll be here with you." It is important for distancers to be able to say, "I'm taking care of myself, but I'm not abandoning you."

SOME COMMUNICATION GUIDELINES

Here are some guidelines for asking for contact, or for privacy.

1. Find out what works. Try saying to your partner, "I have something I really need you to hear, and I'm wondering what is the best way I can say it to you?" Often couples will never have talked to each other about what allows each of them to be more receptive.
2. Avoid surprises. Usually people are more receptive when they have been forewarned. This allows them to relax their automatic defenses and stay more in the present.
3. Ask for what you need instead of complaining. Complaints and blame are invitations for your partner to initiate their part of the script. Making a specific request, such as, "Let's go away this weekend," is usually more effective than one more statement of blame or frustration.
4. Ask as if you expect to get what you want. Tone is at least as important as the words you use. A message that carries a positive, inviting tone has a much better chance of being heard than one like, "I don't suppose you'd like to turn off the game and go on a walk with me."

Anger and pursuit/avoidance are two scripts where the couples have emotional contact at some point, although most of it is negative emotional contact. The next chapter describes two scripts where couples try to avoid emotional contact altogether: the disengaged and the pseudomutual.

6

Emotional
Distance

Two pairs of eyes looking past each other
to different distances.

DENISE LEVERTOV

At first glance the two scripts we will be looking at in this chapter seem completely different. The first, the *pseudomutual*, involves a couple who seem always to be in close, loving contact with each other, while the second, the *disengaged*, involves two people who avoid each other as much as possible.

But this difference is superficial. Both are strategies for avoiding conflict: the pseudomutual by burying all differences; the disengaged by avoiding contact that could create differences. The pseudomutual couple fears that any differences will lead to abandonment, while the disengaged couple fears that closeness will lead to the loss of self. Each script protects the couple by turning down the emotional temperature in the relationship.

Couples who engage in these scripts may seem healthier than couples who engage in anger or pursuit/avoidance, where the conflicts hang out all over, but the core issues that they are organized around can be just as profound. Both partners are likely to be emotionally fragile and vulnerable to the rekindling of childhood wounds. In fact, partners in a disengaged relationship may be so fragile that they have to avoid any issue that consciously or unconsciously reminds them of their childhood.

Of course the main thing these couples avoid is conflict. Unconsciously all emotionally distant couples believe that to differ is to die. Either they learned as children that only feelings that matched their parents' feelings would be mirrored, or they faced their parent's rejection or annihilating anger if they stood up for themselves.

As in the other scripts, the defensive self matches childhood experiences to present-day events. A husband's disapproval of his wife's choice in clothes gets matched with her childhood experience of feeling shame about her body. She might react with defensive anger, and then this anger will, in turn, be matched by her husband with his own childhood experience with an abusive mother. Then their defensive selves will take over and create a script where the husband always compliments his wife's clothes, whether he really feels it or not (pseudomutual), or he stops noticing what she's wearing altogether (disengaged).

EMOTIONAL DISTANCE

Unlike pursuit/avoidance or anger scripts, which involve lots of tension, life for the disengaged and pseudomutual couples is emotionally flat. These couples fear emotional overload—they fear that if they allow their real selves to meet, they will be overwhelmed.

It is my impression that the level of disengagement in today's marriages is increa_ing, if for no other reason then the drastic change in lifestyle brought on by both partners working full-time. Many couples who are trying to manage a household, two jobs, and whatever outside interests and friends they can still maintain find themselves too overwhelmed for much intimacy. They want "peace at all costs" or they want to be left alone. Add children to this equation and the problems increase exponentially. Couples with young children are often too busy keeping body and soul together to have much left over for each other, especially if they are going to have to address conflicts or deep-seated problems.

Even beyond the pressures of modern life, disengaged couples tend to keep busy. They fill their leisure time with projects in or outside the home, or they see friends and entertain a lot. Many times they are disengaged from their own selves as well as from each other. Walt Whitman's line from *Leaves of Grass*, "I loaf and invite my soul" would be lost on them. Their motto is more like "We vacuum or work in the garage to avoid our souls ever meeting."

With intimacy on the back burner, couples gradually grow apart and lose their ability to communicate and problem solve. Little gripes get buried; big problems are best left unsaid for fear of rocking an already shaky boat. The result is a gradual accumulation of resentment and anger. These resentments get stored away in an airtight room. This room begins to feel like dangerous territory—any little spark could ignite a full-out explosion—so then there's more and more reason to avoid conflicts, and more feelings get stored away. It's a self-perpetuating cycle. Disengaged couples drift farther apart. They begin to feel a kind of malaise in the relationship, but they have no words to articulate it. The partners get involved in their separate lives. Often it is the children that become the only place they overlap, but sometimes they are disengaged even from their own children.

Sometimes this type of disengagement breaks down along sex-role stereotypes. The wife may be involved with the house and the children, the husband with his job. The staggering statistics about how much television American families watch support the idea that this script is quite common.

Pseudomutual couples redouble their efforts to patch over growing conflicts with actions: they buy things together, go places, socialize. They try desperately to act like "happy campers" while more and more conflicts get buried.

ORIGIN OF DISENGAGED RELATIONSHIPS

There is a wonderful example of the way couples become disengaged in the recent novel *Love in the Time of Cholera* by the Colombian writer and Nobel Laureate Gabriel García Márquez. In this novel a single trivial incident leads to a lifetime of disengagement. Dr. Juvenal Urbino complains to his young wife, Fermina Daza, that there was no soap in the bathroom when he went to take his shower. Fermina, who sees herself as having to be perfect, can't bear this criticism, and maintains bitterly that her husband is mistaken. Unable to stand this conflict, Juvenal simply moves into another bedroom for several months. Finally, overcome by loneliness, he crawls in beside her in the middle of the night, whispers "There was soap" and they go to sleep. But from this time on each partner moves in separate worlds. Because they could not resolve even the simplest of conflicts, disengagement became a way of survival.

In addition to the fear of conflict, there are four other sources of disengaged relationships: too rigid boundaries; traumatic experiences which the couple can't handle; fear of childhood wounds repeating; and fear of failure. Let's look at each of them in turn.

Boundaries

The term *boundary* refers here to the distinction between yourself and another person. Too rigid boundaries keep others out and make intimacy impossible; too porous boundaries lead to relationships where it is unclear where one person begins and the other leaves off. Healthy boundaries provide both a sense that your inner world is uniquely your own and, at the same time, that it can be knowable to another person. You may note that these two experiences are the opposite of intrusion and abandonment.

Boundaries are formed in childhood, largely through the experience of the boundary between child and parent. When a parent provides a self-delineating experience in response to the child's emotion, the child learns that the emotion exists inside him. Let's take a very simple example: a baby bangs a rattle, and the mother gives a delighted, appreciative look. The baby feels, "I have this delighted, excited feeling inside me and my mother recognizes it." Now the baby grabs the mother's face and pinches, the mother grimaces and pushes his hand away. The baby feels, "I have this curious, excited feeling about pinching my mother's face, but she does not share it, she has a different feeling than me." It is through the accumulation of countless learning experiences like these that the child learns what is inside him and what is inside another person.

All intimate relationships involve a sharing of two subjective worlds. For disengaged couples this sharing feels dangerous. Obviously, they fear that if they share their emotional world they will be intruded on. But they also fear being overwhelmed by having their unmet mirroring needs awakened. Because of these fears they have learned, like the farmers in Robert Frost's poem, that "good fences make good neighbors." Only rigid boundaries will keep them safe from intrusion, and the resulting emotional isolation is an acceptable price for that safety.

Traumatic Experiences

When one of the partners in a relationship experiences profound emotional pain, such as the loss of a loved one or an illness, the marital system is stressed, and the couple may revert to time-worn defenses. Distancers will find subtle ways to not be present; mergers will get overly involved. The other partner may want to be supportive, but may fear being overwhelmed by the mate's emotions and problems. When both partners share a traumatic experience, such as the loss or illness of a child, defensive scripts become almost inevitable. In turning to each other for mirroring and soothing, both are likely to be disappointed, since both are likely to be overwhelmed and needy. This disappointment can lead to a gradual withdrawal. The couple stops discussing their pain, and they drift apart.

I knew a couple who'd lost their home in a fire. At first they tried to band together, but the husband's way of coping was to keep busy, not to seek or offer support. He took care of his grief about their loss by getting involved in working with contractors to rebuild the house, while the wife, in defense against the abandonment, threw herself into helping the children relocate in their new home and school. When their house was finally rebuilt, they found that they could not rebuild their relationship. They had become alienated from each other and unable to talk about the experience that had shattered their comfortable life.

Childhood Wounds

Families that had rigid boundaries and poor communication are perfect places to learn this type of script. Children from such families may never have learned how to get their needs met in relationships, or even that they have needs. Repeating the pattern of disengagement feels perfectly natural. A child from a family that was enmeshed or constantly embroiled in conflict can also come to see this script as a welcome respite. These children experienced constant intrusion from their family. To them rigid boundaries can seem better than no boundaries at all.

Fear of Failure

Disengagement is often caused by the accumulation of small relationship disappointments. A typical scenario involves a couple in the honeymoon phase coming upon a conflict that feels threatening to them. This can be a revelation of some difference—such as a difference over a philosophy or politics, or a disagreement over issues with one of the partner's families. This can feel like a rupture of the oneness of the honeymoon phase. Their inability to resolve the issue and restore the togetherness can fill them with a feeling that their relationship is failing. A couple on their way to a disengaged script will try to cover up such a conflict as quickly as possible. They will make a mutual agreement not to talk about a certain area. As more and more conflicts arise, more and more areas become off limits, and as this happens fewer and fewer safe areas are left open to discussion. Because both partners fear conflict, it becomes safer to just be separate.

PSEUDOMUTUAL RELATIONSHIPS

You probably know a couple who follows the pseudomutual script. They're the people who always say "we" instead of "me," as in "We don't like fancy restaurants." They hold hands and hold the same opinions; for them the honeymoon phase doesn't end, it just blends into the present. The pseudomutual relationship is an attempt to recreate the childhood feelings of oneness, but to maintain it neither partner can grow up and individuate. The poet William Blake said, "Without contraries, there is no progression," but the pseudomutual couple fears "contraries" so much that they are willing to settle for a static relationship.

In the pseudomutual script, each partner's defensive self flees from closeness, where there might be conflict or disappointment, into a fantasy of perfect oneness. To them separateness itself feels like abandonment. If they differ they fear it will lead to a rupture. The disengaged script protects a couple from intrusion, while the pseudomutual script deals with fears of abandonment. Partners who are prone to pseudomutual relationships never got mirrored enough as children. They cover this wound with a bandaid: in place of accurate mirroring they substitute merely being agreed with.

Of course, as with all protective scripts, the pseudomutual one doesn't meet and heal unmet childhood needs. The pseudomutual script only substitutes the deadness of seeming closeness for the aliveness and risk of real intimacy.

A parent who properly mirrors her child says, in effect, "Go off and become your own person, with your own ideas and preferences, and I will delight in your individuality." Couples living the pseudomutual script say to each other instead, "I delight in the way you're like me." There's a missing ingredient; it's like a cake that doesn't rise. But it tastes enough like cake to stop the appetite for real mirroring, and thus protects each partner from re-living the wounds of faulty childhood mirroring.

The pseudomutual is a highly enmeshed script, and you might think that an enmeshed family would predispose a person to this script in adulthood, but this is not always the case. Isn't there something a little lonely about a couple who are always together? In their fear of being alone, loneliness is always present, almost like a ghost. Adults who felt lonely as children might seek to compensate for this by creating a pseudomutual script, but, in avoiding real intimacy, they are replicating their childhood feelings—they remain haunted by loneliness. And they don't dare turn on the lights and chase the ghost away.

MIKE AND RITA

Couples engaged in the pseudomutual script rarely seek counseling, for obvious reasons. If you fear difference and conflict, the last thing you'll want is to learn to communicate individual needs and differences more clearly. More often I see such couples when something has gone awry, and the pseudomutual script has been broken off. The event that breaks this script can be as major as the revelation of an affair, or merely the emergence of some incontrovertible difference between the couple.

Mike and Rita's crisis came when Mike decided to turn down a chance to become a partner in his law firm. A two-career family, they had shared being ambitious and enjoyed the material things success could buy. For Mike this decision was the first time in his life he'd ever really made a choice that was his own. To his wife it was a betrayal.

I had to reconstruct their script by taking a detailed history of their relationship. When Mike and Rita came in they were without a script that worked for them. They alternated between the anger of mutual recriminations and the disengagement of sullen silences. They were scared and deeply shaken, and for good reason: neither

Mike nor Rita knew how conflicts could be talked about or negotiated. Underneath her rage, Rita felt like a terrible failure. She saw her job in the relationship as managing all problems, being on top of everything, and always being cheery. The thing that troubled her most about Mike's decision was that he hadn't consulted her before making it. Mike was equally surprised by the strength of Rita's reaction—he wondered if she had some kind of hormone imbalance or was having a nervous breakdown. Their pseudo-mutual script had worked so well that neither one really knew the other. Rita had no idea that underneath Mike's career-building conformity there was a part of him that yearned to do something creative or adventurous, and Mike had no idea that Rita was terrified of surprises.

Here's what I gathered of their history. When Mike met Rita he was just out of college, feeling adrift and on the rebound from a relationship that had begun in high school and continued on and off for five years. He felt that she was almost a miracle: bright, pretty, with definite ideas of who she was and where she was going. Rita was finishing a business program at a prestigious college, and was actively being recruited by several companies.

In some ways, Mike was Rita's "project." After he met her, he got a job as an accountant and began attending law school at night. They began to pursue the urban good life with a vengeance. They spent a lot of time fixing up their house, and they were very supportive of each other's careers. They consciously cultivated the same interests, including art and music.

Underneath this script they were two deeply dependent and scared people who were in strong denial of these feelings. Trying to be a perfect couple was their way of seeking some protection from unconsciously held childhood wounds. It is not uncommon for couples to substitute one kind of need for another when they form adult relationships. In Mike and Rita's case, they compensated for the mirroring failures in their childhood by trying to be idealizable to each other.

Rita felt that her parents' marriage was "near perfect," and her parents seemed to her to be everything one should strive to be. And strive she did: her whole life had been devoted to living up to some vague sense she had of her parents' expectations. She secretly lived with a fear that she could never be as good as her mother.

Beneath the outward perfection of her family Rita had a childhood of severe deprivation and loneliness: no one but an occasional housekeeper had every really been there for Rita when she felt less than "perfect." No one had ever really consoled her when she felt sad or set limits when she was angry or out of control. Instead Rita had learned to control herself, to always be composed and in charge. And she learned to really be good at helping other people with their problems. This was a way of never letting anyone (including herself) see that she had a problem. As long as she could stay in control and avoid surprises, this worked fairly well for her.

It would have been easy to write Rita off as a rather shallow, materialistic person, but I could see that all this striving for physical perfection was a defense against a lot of pain. I could also see that she really loved Mike; he was probably the only person she'd ever been close to.

Mike did not have any illusions about his parents' marriage or his family life. His parents had divorced when he was 3 and his father had moved to another city. His mother worked hard to provide a very comfortable lifestyle for him, yet she seemed to have been quite depressed. Given this level of family-of-origin disengagement, Rita's affection did seem like a miracle. But Mike unconsciously resented the price he had to pay for this affection, and he was unconscious of the source of this resentment in feelings toward his emotionally withdrawn mother.

It never did become clear to me what exactly prompted Mike to turn down the promotion. Perhaps he was scared of failure, perhaps a piece of his real self emerged to let him know his heart wasn't in it, or perhaps he was motivated by a desire to finally defy Rita's expectations. It was probably a combination of all three. He was enraged at Rita's reaction to his job choice, and before he could sit back and look at where that anger was coming from, he had to just get it out:

"I can't believe your reaction. Here for the first time in my life I make a choice that is what I want to do, and all you can think of is yourself. All you can talk about is how betrayed you feel. Well, I feel damned betrayed too. I thought that you really loved me, and wanted me to get what I wanted in life. Now I feel that all you want is for me to be a good drone who gives you the things you want."

This was strong medicine, but it needed to come out. The anger that was surfacing had been submerged beneath their pseudo-mutual script. Sometimes we have no choice but to work through our confusion between our partner and our parent. This was true for Mike. He needed to express his anger at Rita before he could get at what was underneath it. Mike was not being completely fair to Rita, but they had both been protecting each other from anger far too long for it to come out fairly. Daniel Wile, who has done some important work on anger in couples, points out that couples can't always get their anger out in the best ways. Sometimes the anger has to come out and then the couple has to recover from it before they can move ahead.

Rita was at first taken aback by Mike's anger, but eventually she was able to confront him with anger of her own: "How could I support you when I feel like I hardly even know you. We've been together all these years and you never expressed any dissatisfaction with your job or with our life. I feel like our marriage is a sham, I feel that we've just been going through the motions. I don't know who you are and I don't know how to trust you anymore."

I let this kind of interchange go on a while before I intervened. Both partners felt that this incident revealed terrible truths about each other. Mike felt that Rita was someone who didn't care about his happiness, and Rita felt that Mike had tricked her and never let her see who he really was. Both of these feelings were out of proportion to what happened, which is that Mike turned down a promotion and Rita freaked out about it. This showed me that the issue was as much symbolic as actual. In my experience, when couples are aroused by symbols and begin saying things to each other like "you always" or "you never," it means that something has made them feel like children again, reacting to something their parents did to hurt them.

It took a while for the connections to be made, but eventually both Mike and Rita were able to see what this incident symbolized for each of them. When I asked Rita what it felt like for her to find out that she didn't really know someone she was so close to, she said, "I feel that everything is caving in. It's a terrible feeling." When I wondered aloud if the loss of her sense of who Mike was resembled in any way her disillusionment with her mother, she realized how much she "needed to believe that my mother was perfect. If I didn't I'd have to let in how totally alone I felt." As long as Mike acted in safe, predictable ways, Rita never had to feel those kind of feelings. She needed to be in control, and he let her control him.

What was at stake here for Rita was a phenomenon that Heinz Kohut called *traumatic deidealization*. Everyone needs to replace their childhood idealized view of their parents with a more realistic one. Usually this happens gradually, and some of the glow of the idealized feeling is preserved. But Rita had protected her need for an idealizable parent by denying her own feelings of loneliness. Her traumatic deidealizing experience of Mike now was being generalized to a loss of her secure picture of her perfect mother.

I wondered if Mike's decision to refuse the promotion wasn't, at least unconsciously, an attempt to send a message to Rita that he was tired of protecting her by living up to her expectations, and that he wanted mirroring from her for his inner life, not his outer actions. At first Mike denied that his decision had anything at all to do with Rita, but later he saw that this was true. "I didn't realize it at the time, but maybe I was trying to provoke a response out of Rita when I turned down the promotion. Maybe I wanted to see if for once someone could be excited just for me."

Mike's decision not to take the promotion prompted a growthful crisis in their relationship, one that forced both of them to look at the emptiness their pseudomutual script was masking. Painful as it was, it became the opportunity for them to begin doing a lot of work on themselves and on their relationship. They floundered for some time after that incident, sometimes going back to their pseudomutual script, other times falling into bitter arguments, but slowly they developed more intimacy in their lives. Mike became aware that if he were to get Rita to mirror his real self's plans and dreams, he would have to let her see them, and Rita began to see that not all surprises or emotions were fearful. Nothing's really changed outwardly for them. Mike's still with the same firm, he's just decided that the sixty-hour weeks required of partners aren't for him. He didn't run off to Tahiti with a set of paints and an easel.

I hadn't seen Mike and Rita in some time, but I got a call from Rita the other day. She was thinking of going to school to study psychology, with an eventual goal of becoming a therapist herself, and wanted my advice on graduate programs in our area. Mike's pursuit of goals that met his real self's needs evidently had given Rita permission to do the same.

MAKING CONTACT

The hurt and blame of anger scripts or the inherent unhappiness of the pursuit/avoidance script can potentially lead a couple to their real selves. Unless their script breaks down, it is difficult for emotionally distant couples to find the clues that can lead back to the childhood needs and fears that are controlling them. Without a crisis, their work to improve their relationship has to begin almost by faith—faith that the vague sense of emptiness that underlies the disengaged couple or the obsessive pursuit of happiness that underlies the pseudomutual couple mask something essential about themselves and their relationship.

The first act of faith is to admit that you have needs that go beyond safety and admiration—like the need for someone to understand your struggles and your sadness. It may be hard to acknowledge that what's going on inside is not a one-note samba but a symphony of different feelings, much less to get in touch with your longings for a response to those varied tones. The key to understanding disengaged relationships is in acknowledging that we do not outgrow the child inside who wanted to be smiled at when he was proud and comforted when he was sad. The shame that distant couples feel about these "childish" dependency needs makes them doubly hard to access.

Disengaged couples must make a conscious effort to bring those feelings into the relationship. I've had partners keep journals of their various emotional highs and lows, and then share them with each other. Finding and sharing the moments in each day when you needed comfort and understanding becomes a kind of practice.

TOLERATING CONFLICT

Conflicts inevitably arise as you try to express more of your feelings and needs with your partner. Will he mirror your feelings or disappoint you? If she does disappoint you, will the relationship tolerate your anger about the disappointment? Will he become competitive, believing that, if he meets your needs, his own won't be met?

Emotionally distant couples believe that such conflicts will destroy the tie that keeps them together. There is a paradox to the protection their script has offered them: since their defense is to keep the tie vague or one dimensional, they have not tested it in conflict and have no idea how strong it really is.

Safety becomes the first priority in learning to tolerate conflict. You must make a firm commitment to stay together before you can be safe expressing your disappointments. You must start slowly, with non-threatening issues, in order to build up confidence. I know one husband in a disengaged relationship who wanted to tell his wife about his sexual frustrations. He was sincerely interested in making more contact by expressing his needs and feelings, but he had no idea how devastating this would be for his wife, who unconsciously believed that no one would love her if she did not meet all their needs. They were trying to run with conflict before they knew how to walk.

Another part of safety around conflict is to have agreed-on "circuit breakers" in place. Both partners must have the right to break off a discussion or argument if it gets to be too much to handle. This can be especially difficult, because if you start to get in touch with your real feelings it is painful to stop. You feel that your childhood trauma of having your real feelings suppressed is repeating itself. For this reason an agreement to break off a discussion must be accompanied by an agreement to switch it back on at an agreed upon later time, preferably not too far in the future.

Perhaps more than any of the others, changing the disengaged and pseudomutual scripts involves conscious effort, but since there is an inherent symmetry in these relationships (both partners are distancers), there is a good possibility for empathy and forgiveness.

With our discussion of the disengaged and the pseudomutual, we have completed our survey of the four basic scripts. We will discuss how to change these scripts in Chapter 9. First we will explore some common areas of conflict for couples, beginning with sex and intimacy.

7

Sex
and
Intimacy

Body of my woman I will live on through your marvel-
   ousness.
My thirst, my desire without end, my wavering road!
Dark river beds down which the eternal thirst is flowing,
And the fatigue is flowing, and the grief without shore.
                                          PABLO NERUDA

Since the sexual revolution of the sixties, our society has been increasingly open about sex. Television shows routinely feature sexual themes, and sex manuals are sold at supermarkets. Yet, for all this openness, sex remains a problem area for many couples. I see couples who complain that their sexual interest is decreasing, or couples in which one partner complains that the other is neglectful or unresponsive sexually. Sometimes their sexual complaints have led to affairs, threatening the life of the relationship.

When these couples turn to books or magazines for advice, they are likely to find information about the physical aspects of sex. Try a new position, these books advise, or go on a romantic vacation. The greatest beneficiaries of such advice are likely to be chiropractors and travel agents, because, for the majority of sexually troubled couples, the problem has more to do with psychological issues of intimacy, rooted in their invisible marriage. All that the emphasis on technique and performance does is make many couples feel inadequate, as if something were physically wrong with them.

Some sexual problems do arise from an organic base or as a side effect to medication, so a thorough medical checkup should always be the first step. Problems such as premature ejaculation, impotence, or extreme fear of sex require specialized treatment, even if there is no physiological component. This treatment can often take place in a couples context and include work on issues of intimacy as well as the specific sexual dysfunction.

Many couples' sex lives never recover from the waning of the initial intensity. The fact that intimacy has to be created, instead of surrendered to, is disappointing, even wounding, to many couples. Part of the lure of sex is that its effortlessness can recreate a childhood feeling of being allowed to play, rather than having to take responsibility. Planning for sex, getting a babysitter, talking about needs and fears can feel like an intrusion on childhood joy. Of course, if joy actually was continually intruded upon in childhood, sex, like other emotionally painful experiences, becomes part of a script of struggle or disengagement.

Though there may not be any quick fix for a disappointing sex life, there are very real things you can do to improve your level of sexual satisfaction. You can come to see sex as part of a pattern of intimacy and deal with the issues that are making intimacy difficult. These might be unresolved current conflicts: a sink full of dirty dishes is probably more detrimental to a couple's sex life than a few extra pounds or gray hairs. The problems may be part of a defensive script that provides protection by avoiding sexual intimacy. Though the myths of what novelist Erica Jong called the "zipless" sexual encounter persist, sex in relationship is a part of everything that happens in a couple's life. To change a protective script around sexuality, you must come to understand why it is there in the first place, and then consciously recreate the safety you need for greater sexual intimacy to flourish.

THE PSYCHOLOGICAL ASPECTS OF SEX

Freud noted that sexual intimacy involved a kind of return to childhood. Like children, lovers are playful, pleasure oriented, and free of time constraints and responsibilities. Our language reflects this: lovers call each other "baby" and coo at each other. Sex involves surrender to another—in the release of orgasm we are completely at our partner's mercy. This surrender resembles a child's relationship with his parent. At the extreme of sexual bliss, we may feel like a young child, completely safe in our mother's arms. Freud saw in our longing for sexual union a yearning to return to the perfect sense of oneness we once felt with our mother. When it works, sexual union can provide a healing for lives that are isolated and cut off from this sense of oneness.

But the peril of such regression is that, rather than return us to the peaceful memory of oneness, it can return us to painful memories of intrusion, abandonment, or shame. Sexual arousal is a highly charged, expansive feeling. When we look to our partner to respond to this expansive feeling, we are replaying the childhood longing for mirroring and idealizing. We want our partner to be right there with us in our bliss, (mirroring) and we want him to know what we want without our having to say it (idealizing). An experience of our lover not being right there with us or not knowing what we want can remind us of times when we needed our parent's understanding and responsiveness but didn't get it. If our partner makes too many demands in bed, it may remind us of times when our parents' own needs intruded on our childhood world of sensual pleasure.

Of course, no lovers are perfect, and such feelings of abandonment or intrusion are inevitable. The problem comes when our defensive self, sensing a pattern in the present that matches serious childhood wounds of intrusion or abandonment, takes over and institutes its fight-or-flight response. Then an incident that is in present time only an annoyance or a frustration triggers an overpowering feeling of anger or fear. Rather than communicating these feelings, we are more likely to start a fight or to flee from intimacy completely. Many women complain that their men want to go to sleep or get up right after sex. For them, afterplay is as important as foreplay. For a woman who has a core issue of abandonment, however, the absence of such attention from her partner may remind her of childhood trauma. She may feel like Wendy from Chapter 5, who ran into her mother's room bursting with excitement about what her piano teacher had told her, only to be dismissed by her mother's icy stare. If this happens repeatedly, she may come to feel that the pain of this abandonment feeling outweighs the pleasure of sex, and she may try to avoid sexual intimacy altogether.

Sex can feel intrusive to people who have core issues around guilt and obligation. The gift of sexual pleasure feels like a baited hook. Like Wendy's husband Lee, who always felt that his mother's affection carried a hidden message of "I'm taking care of you so that you will later take care of me," we may come to feel that accepting our partner's sexual affection may obligate us to take care of her later, whether we want to or not. Fear of intrusion will lead us to avoid sexual intimacy, or to create a fight around some sexual issue in order to prevent feeling controlled. When a man says "I really like such and such, but she refuses to do it," he is often defending against his fear of being controlled by trying to control his partner.

SHAME

We discussed the connection between shame and sexuality in Chapter 2. Shame is very related to bodily excitement. We may long for a partner to help free us of long-held feelings of shame about bodily excitement. At the same time we may also fear that he or she will reinforce them. When we lose ourselves in physical excitement, we are especially vulnerable to shame-inducing surprises or rejection.

Many children received shame-inducing messages about their bodies. They were told not to touch their genitals. Girls were told to wear a top, even as very young children, though their brothers ran around in just a pair of shorts. These messages were delivered as ultimatums, with no explanation attached.

Most of us arrive at relationship with fears of inadequacy we long to have dispelled. Women worry if their breasts are the right size and if their bodies fit the proper image of attractiveness. Men obsess about the size of their penises. Women worry that their physical desire or excitement is shameful, and often hide it behind safer fantasies of romance and marriage.

Men in particular are often ashamed about their sexual performance. Experiences of impotence and premature ejaculation can lead to pervasive shame about sexuality. When one client came to me for treatment of cocaine addiction, we discovered that his drug use was connected to sexual shame: he had been impotent during his first sexual experience (which was under the bleachers during a high school gym dance, a situation that would probably make most men have problems). He had been so ashamed that he developed a strategy: from now on he would always use drugs before sex. Sometimes the drugs would allow him to be potent, but more importantly, when they didn't, they allowed him a face-saving excuse. He could say to his partner, "I'm too stoned now." Other men become workaholics, blame their partners ("She doesn't turn me on anymore"), or channel their sexuality into fantasies or pornography in order to avoid potentially shameful encounters.

In addition to shame about bodies and performance, there is also the shame of dependency. Partners don't want to be exposed as being sexually needy, especially if they are ashamed about leftover childhood needs. Men especially are taught to be ashamed of dependency. They long for the sense of oneness, but at the same time are ashamed to expose their longing. Sex at first becomes an acceptable channel for the expression of these needs, but as we grow more intimate we begin to feel psychologically as well as physically naked.

When sex brings up feelings of shame, abandonment, and intrusion, we are likely to respond defensively. When two people are responding with their defensive selves, the result is a repetitive script that binds up sexual anxiety in a pattern of anger or avoidance.

ANGER IN THE BEDROOM

Since sex makes us vulnerable to injuries to the self, it can be a trigger to defensive anger. Some couples fight about sex, while others use anger about other issues to avoid sex altogether. Unlike the myth of a couple fighting just so they can romantically make up, for most couples anger is a real turn-off. Hurt feelings and bitterness usually prevent the kind of surrender that makes good sex possible. In anger scripts that involve sex, blame predominates. "She's frigid," the man may accuse. "He makes love like a mechanic fixing a car," the woman will retaliate. "You didn't complain when you met me," he'll reply, "or were you just faking it so you could hook me?"

Sometimes it is hard for me to remember that two people expressing such bitterness are really responding to fear and that underneath this bitterness there may be an active bond between the couple. By asking couples to pinpoint when their romantic life began to deteriorate, I can discover the time that the couple realized the risk of sexual closeness and instituted the anger script to prevent getting hurt. I usually find an underlying issue of abandonment or intrusion beneath the loss of intimacy.

ALAN AND JAN

Alan and Jan went on a world trip after they met. When they returned, they decided to stay with Jan's parents while they got on their feet. Jan had a secret agenda: she wanted Alan to join her father's business, and she hoped that if they got to know each other this would happen. Unfortunately, it was just the opposite. The father and son-in-law saw each other as rivals. They began to argue a lot and respond to each other sarcastically. Jan saw herself caught in the middle, while Alan felt that she always sided with her father.

Both partners felt that their sex life started to deteriorate when they stayed with her parents. They thought it was a lack of privacy that kept them apart. They did not know why their bitter fights had taken the place of sexual contact, and they did not know the invisible dimensions of the triangle between Jan, her father and Alan.

Alan's own father had died when he was 10, and two years later his mother remarried. His stepfather was much more successful than his father had been, and tried to win the boy's affection with material things. The boy, out of loyalty to his father, resisted. Rather than understand the loyalty dilemma Alan was in, his mother grew exasperated with him. She feared that her new husband would grow impatient, so she pressured him to open up to his stepfather. This created issues of both abandonment and intrusion for him: abandonment because his mother wasn't being understanding of his feelings; intrusion because she tried to get him to feel the way she wanted him to.

The situation at his in-laws' resembled this childhood scenario very closely. Jan played the part of his mother, trying to facilitate a connection between him and yet another father figure. Once again he felt betrayed by a woman he was counting on. As we have said, the very nature of sex lends itself to a replay of these kind of parental transferences. Rather than let himself be "mothered" by Jan in bed, Alan's defensive self took over and replaced their former intimacy with a pattern of fighting. Their honeymoon phase of world travel and adventure had given way to bitter fights.

For Jan and Alan, the way out of this problem wasn't in recreating the excitement of their world trip. The innocence of those days was gone forever. The way out was in working through the underlying issues. When Alan got in touch with the way he felt Jan had betrayed him when she sided with her father, he grew tremendously angry. This anger touched into his childhood pain. Twenty years of rage came pouring out as he generalized his anger at women, calling them gold-diggers and opportunists. It was necessary for Alan to express this anger to get beyond it and, fortunately, Jan was smart enough not to take it personally and respond in kind. In fact, she reported that she actually was feeling closer to Alan. "At least I know what he's angry about. It's better than those irrational tirades he used to have." For Alan, Jan's ability to listen to his anger was tremendously important. He felt that at last someone really understood him and cared about what he was feeling.

Jan and Alan were able to replace their defensive-self anger with anger that expressed their real selves. As part of their healing process, Jan had to express her anger at the way Alan had been abusive over the past few years, but expressing this anger cleared the way for a fresh encounter. Alan began to see Jan as someone whom he could trust, not someone who would betray him the way his mother had, and Jan began to see Alan as a sensitive human being, not an angry bully. While this did not lead to a second honeymoon with bells and fireworks, it did lead to a greatly improved sex life, with a sense of peace and security for both of them. Jan described the changes this way: "It's not that we've stopped fighting. But the fights don't escalate to the point where that's all we're doing. It used to be that we wouldn't want to touch each other for days or even weeks afterward. Now we'll feel like making up or even making love the same day." Their anger had stopped being part of a script that protected them from risking sexual intimacy.

COLD ASHES IN THE HEARTH: THE SEXUALLY DISENGAGED COUPLE

While sexual libido varies widely, couples who find themselves in nonsexual relationships are probably suffering emotional disengagement as well. Sometimes this disengagement has evolved from a pursuit/avoidance script, when the pursuer just gave up. Other times both partners are avoidant because they have childhood issues that led them to fear intimacy. Sometimes something so traumatic has happened in the life of a couple that that they have given up trying to be close for fear of being hurt again. This last is often true of couples who have survived an affair.

Whatever the origin, once a sexually disengaged script gets going it tends to have a life of its own. The defensive self takes over and keeps us fleeing, and the real self's desire for pleasure and closeness gets lost. It becomes a vicious cycle: the lack of sexual intimacy causes hurt feelings, and these hurt feelings make it harder to be sexually close.

The best way to break such a script is to go through the hurt feelings that caused it in the first place. But couples often fear "dredging up the past." They feel that they've gotten along reasonably well so far, and wonder if talking about the hurt is worth the risk of making a stable situation unstable. In addition, one or both of the partners may feel shame about their sexual inadequacy. Couples who have given up on sex are often the most fearful and wounded of all. At least with pursuit and avoidance or anger scripts, there is some movement around sex, even if the end result is not greater satisfaction. The challenge that disengaged couples face is for one or both partners to risk initiating change.

For the great majority of couples I see, the resulting improvement in communication far outweighs the risks. They find, despite their fear and hurt, that forgiveness is possible, and that the candle of sexual passion can indeed burn a second time.

JOAN AND PETER

Joan and Peter had been married for seventeen years when they came to me for couples therapy. Peter was a researcher at a local medical school who had done important work on a childhood disease, and Joan was the assistant director of a local charitable foundation. They seemed markedly insecure when they spoke about themselves and their relationship, despite their considerable success in their respective careers.

One source of their insecurity was revealed when they disclosed that they hadn't had sex in over two years. Though they still felt affection for each other, they believed that the breakdown in their sex life meant that they would eventually break up. They both felt ashamed of their sexual problems, and had never told anyone about them.

Both Joan and Peter thought that they had specific sexual problems. Peter felt that he was just not motivated, and wondered if he had something physically wrong. However, when he consulted a doctor no physical problems surfaced. Joan blamed herself for the problem. She felt that sex made her nervous, that it made her hands and feet perspire, and that this turned Peter off. As it turned out, the sexual problems were rooted not in physical issues such as sex drive or specific physiological responses, but in issues of abandonment, intrusion, and shame that were part of a larger picture of relationship patterns and childhood issues.

Joan's cultural and family background contributed to her feelings about sex and intimacy. Joan's father was a kindly, ineffectual man who had met Joan's mother, an East Indian, while he worked for the Foreign Service. Joan's mother was a nervous, controlling woman who feared abandonment. Her cultural dislocation made these fears greater. Joan saw her father as enslaved by her mother's moods. Whenever Joan did something to upset her mother, such as stay out too late or wear clothes she disapproved of, her mother would complain that Joan had "ruined everything." So Joan learned as a child that doing things for herself could destroy her mother's tranquility and lead to a disruption in the family. Her mother would often sulk for days when she was upset. Joan formed an unconscious belief that if she let herself have her own life, she would hurt her mother and, in turn, be abandoned.

Sexual intimacy with Peter brought up the fear of repeating this pattern. When Joan surrendered to sexual excitement, her unconscious mind became anxious that she would be punished for having her own pleasure and not thinking of someone else. When this anxiety made her feet and hands perspire, she felt that Peter was turned off and this reinforced the belief that she had "ruined everything" and Peter would soon abandon her.

This belief became a self-fulfilling prophecy when Joan's issues combined with Peter's to form their invisible marriage. Despite the ethnic differences (Peter's family was New England Protestant), Peter's childhood issues were remarkably similar to Joan's. His father, a businessman, was a kind man, but was completely wrapped up in his work. Peter's mother was a dynamic and powerful woman whose many enthusiasms hid her underlying insecurity and loneliness in her marriage. Peter longed to be closer to his father, but his father did not have time for him. Instead, Peter became caught up in his mother's world of art, music, and culture. Unconsciously, he felt the requirement that he participate in his mother's world to be an intrusion and a threat to his developing sense of maleness. He was required to mirror her, rather than having his emerging male energy mirrored. Peter's defense against this intrusion was to retreat into his own world of silence and solitude.

When they would start to make love and Joan would grow anxious, it triggered childhood issues for both of them. Peter felt that he had to take care of Joan's anxiety by stopping his own pleasure and reassuring her. He had to give up the wish to have his own excitement mirrored by Joan, and he also had to give up his own thoughts and feelings, which were that he didn't really care for sweaty feet, and pretend that they didn't bother him. In order to defend himself against the intrusive requirement that he take care of Joan, he would withdraw emotionally. Part of his withdrawal was into an active and private world of sexual fantasies. This withdrawal triggered Joan's fear of abandonment and further reinforced her belief that she had ruined everything. These issues, coupled with the shame they felt for not living up to some standard of sexual frequency, led to a complete breakdown in their sex life.

The key to breaking this cycle of sexual disengagement was communication. With my encouragement, Peter was able to express his real feelings about Joan's anxiety: "I hate your sweaty palms and feet. They're a real turn-off." Peter came to realize that the real turn-off was feeling like he had to protect Joan at the expense of his own self-expression. Being able to express these negative feelings also allowed him to sincerely express some positive ones, such as how much he liked Joan's figure and how much he missed their intimacy.

Peter was surprised that his negative feelings about Joan's sweaty appendages did not destroy her. In fact, she was able to laugh and say, "I hate them too." It turned out she would rather that Peter stay close and express his real feelings than alternate between acting protective and then abandoning her.

After working at expressing these feelings and talking about the hurt feelings that had led to their two-year abstinence, Joan and Peter felt that they were ready to try and resume intimacy. Because so much was riding on this, I told them that I thought the first step was to have bad, perfunctory sex. I suggested that they try out the hypothesis that bad sex was better than no sex. I hoped to relieve them of performance anxiety, and to help them not feel ashamed if things didn't go right. They found that, free of some of the emotional baggage of their invisible marriage, they were able to enjoy sex more and feel closer to each other than at any time in their long relationship. They bought a house in the country, and began having romantic retreats on the weekends.

PURSUIT/AVOIDANCE: THE SEXUAL MERRY-GO-ROUND

Many couples come in complaining that one partner is unavailable or unresponsive sexually. These couples resemble horses on a merry-go-round: when one of them is up sexually, the other is down. While the stereotype is a horny or oversexed man chasing a frigid or unresponsive woman, I have found that men and women find their partners sexually unavailable with about equal frequency.

The pursuer in this script apparently has an enormous appetite for sex and intimacy, while the avoidant partner feels hounded and intruded upon. "He's after me the minute I return from a business trip," one woman complains, "I don't even have a chance to unpack." Meanwhile the pursuer feels angry and neglected. "I try to get his interest every way I can think of," another woman complains, "but he's like a sack of lead the minute he goes to bed. Lately I've started to pick a fight at bedtime, just so I can get his attention."

Both partners keep the script going. The way the pursuer makes advances guarantees that he or she will be rejected, and the way that the avoider acts rigid and rejecting guarantees that the process will escalate. Both partners play their part in seeing that sex is avoided, yet each blames the other without seeing that the way they are initiating sex or the way they are refusing it is part of the problem: "He just grabs me, like I'm a piece of meat," "I feel that she's going to devour me, she's so needy," "It's 'not tonight' the moment I reach for her, even if I'm just caressing her hair," or "He just cuts me off with a grunt that says, 'nobody home.'"

Sometimes a change of tactics will greatly improve a couple's sex life. Often the pursuing partner needs to, in the words of the great Otis Redding song, "try a little tenderness." "I like my shoulders rubbed," one woman was able to tell her partner, "I can get turned on much easier if I let go of some of the stress I'm carrying."

The conditions that allow for the expression of desire may have to be negotiated. "I feel physical contact is a way of getting close emotionally, but she always wants to talk first," says one man. "If she would just be a little more forward physically, I think I'd be much more responsive."

Similarly, the way a "no" is conveyed can make all the difference. "I don't feel like it tonight, but let's get a babysitter this weekend," is a lot easier to hear than an abrupt rejection. Even "I don't want to make love, but I'd love to hug and snuggle," conveys an accepting message.

But for couples whose pursuit/avoidance script reflects protection against childhood pain, such a change of tactics, though useful, will not be sufficient. In these couples both partners need to admit their investment in avoiding intimacy, and both partners need to make conscious efforts to create it.

JOHN AND VICKY

Vicky, a young mother of two, felt that John was always after her, that he would come up behind her when she was doing the dishes and try to hug her, and that, no matter how much she tried to please him sexually, he was never satisfied. John was also given to occasional explosive bursts of anger, which made Vicky want to be even more distant. John, a computer salesman, felt that these outbursts were related to his sexual frustration. He apologized for them, but underneath his apology I could still hear anger that his needs were not getting met. John complained that he had tried almost everything to get Vicky to be more responsive sexually, but nothing had worked.

Many men channel all of their mirroring needs into trying to get a woman to approve of them sexually. It's one of the few culturally sanctioned ways of expressing dependency. Unfortunately, by putting all of his dependency needs in the sexual basket, John was really telegraphing a kind of regressed dependency that is a turn-off to many women, especially to an already overburdened mom like Vicky. Instead of hearing an invitation to pleasure and play, Vicky was hearing in John's advances a demand that she drop everything and take care of him.

Vicky would often ignore John's advances, wiggling out of his embrace and continuing the conversation, or she would stay up late doing laundry or watching TV, knowing that John had to leave early for work and couldn't wait up for her indefinitely. These passive responses made John feel more invisible, and thus more needy and demanding. Part of Vicky's passivity was created by her fear of John's anger, which reminded her of the way her own father had often yelled at her. She had learned as a child that it was better to be passive than to risk an angry confrontation. Vicky's own needs for mirroring from her partner, such as for his appreciation of her efforts at mothering the kids, went unexpressed.

On the surface, John and Vicky's script looked like a real conflict—he wanted sex, she wanted privacy—but, underneath, the script protected them from their core issues: John's unmet needs for mirroring and affirmation and Vicky's fear that asserting her own needs would lead to verbal abuse.

John had grown up in the shadow of his successful and athletic older brother. Rather than compete, John drew inside himself, becoming a skilled woodsman and fisherman. It turned out that John had had several learning disabilities and had floundered in school until they were diagnosed. Even though he eventually did quite well in school, isolation was fixed. In the face of his family's rejection, John's real self withdrew, and his defensive self went along with the protective fantasy that he didn't need anybody.

This lasted until he met Vicky, a beautiful young woman who was working with him at a ski resort in Colorado. The fact that she loved and admired him was a revelation, and mobilized his real self's longings. When their intimacy began to break down, what promised to be a second chance started to seem to John like a repetition of his childhood. To protect himself, he began to pursue Vicky in ways that secretly pushed her away.

As we began to explore their sexual issues, Vicky emphasized the effects that John's violent outbursts had on her. Though they were infrequent, she felt that they caused her to want to shut down sexually. As I asked her to stay with the feeling of being afraid of John, childhood memories of her father's anger began to emerge. Her father would attack her when she tried to defy him or seek more freedom. He knew how to say very hurtful things to Vicky. He would find areas of her vulnerability, like her shyness, and mock them. It may not have seemed like that much abuse to an outside observer, but to Vicky the effect was shattering.

It turned out that sex was a particular area of vulnerability for Vicky, who feared that her yearnings to freely express herself would be thwarted and that she would be mocked and criticized. In fact, John, despite his temper, really tried to be a considerate lover—he didn't hold to macho values, or consider sex his right or privilege—but still Vicky would find herself freezing up.

An exploration of what actually happened for Vicky during foreplay showed the connection to her childhood scenario. At certain moments before sex, she would have what amounted to panic attacks. She would begin breathing very rapidly, and would feel almost faint with anxiety. Surrendering to John sexually made her feel like the little kid who was terrified of surprises: letting go of control around a man flooded her with fear. Because Vicky was not tuned in to these dynamics, she just experienced herself as not being very turned on.

Given Vicky's childhood experiences, it was an absolute necessity for her to feel safe and in control before she could let herself get turned on; even John's mostly gentle insistence on more sex had made her feel that her participation was forced. I emphasized to Vicky that she was absolutely in charge of her own body, and that she had the complete right to say no to John whenever she needed to. This kept sex from being a repetition of times when she had no control over her father's behavior.

I also told Vicky that she was to stop being sexual whenever she had a panic attack. I asked her what she wanted at those times, and she said that she just wanted John to hold her and rock her gently. Between them they agreed on a way for her to signal John that this is what she needed. I also helped John to find ways to check out if Vicky was available for physical contact, even hugging, before he just came up to her.

Rather than being put off by all of this, John was actually relieved. He was very glad that the sexual problems had a possible solution. In fact, John, who had at first seemed rather immature to me, grew in stature as he was able to help Vicky. He saw himself as a protector, not as a rejected little boy.

For Vicky, the results were a revelation. Knowing that she had the right to stop anytime things got uncomfortable made it possible for her to let herself go. "I never thought sex could be like this," she reported.

NEW ROMANCE, NEW INTIMACY

To recreate intimacy in a relationship when it has broken down takes conscious effort. Some couples, faced with this loss of spontaneity, begin to work on their relationship. Too often, this becomes a joyless task. I think the word *work* carries the wrong connotation. Coming to really know your partner, as well as coming to understand your own childhood issues, can be a process filled with the joy of discovery. Maintaining the repetitive script is much closer to drudgery.

The process of creating this new sexual intimacy is exactly the process of creating a conscious, real-self-based relationship. This will almost inevitably open the door to greater physical fulfillment. Typically, as couples embark on resolving their problems in the invisible marriage, they find themselves naturally having more frequent and more pleasurable sex.

The key to the new intimacy and the new romance is communication. While honeymoon romance took you out of yourselves, mature romance brings you more fully into yourselves. Whereas on your honeymoon you wanted your partner to know just what you wanted, the new romance demands that you tell them what you want. On your honeymoon you wanted to achieve perfect oneness; the new romance requires you to be one independent person relating to another independent person. You do not seek to obliterate your individuality in sex, but to fully express it. Sex becomes part of a larger pattern of communication, both verbal and nonverbal. While different couples will come to different agreements around sex, certain commitments, in my experience, are necessary for this new sexual intimacy to flourish.

1. Both you and your partner must agree that sex is always consensual. Neither partner has the right to expect sex as a right or privilege, and neither partner has a duty to have sex for the other's sake.
2. Both you and your partner have a right to control your own bodies. You should not participate against your will in any act that does not feel comfortable or pleasurable to you.
3. Sexual issues should be addressed as part of the whole relationship. The question should not be, "Why aren't we having more sex?" but "Why aren't we feeling closer?"

4. In trying to resolve sexual problems or frustrations, you should look at your own behavior before you blame your partner. You should ask, "How am I keeping the problem going? Am I being too demanding, or asking in the wrong ways? Am I being too much the avoider, or resisting in the wrong ways?"
5. Problems should be resolved through communication rather than manipulation, dumping of anger, or avoiding each other. Talking about sex is essential in maintaining a mature sex life.
6. Being willing to encounter each other sexually can simply mean being willing to become aroused. It is not necessary, or even particularly desirable, for you to wait for arousal to initiate or to respond to sex. Mature couples can learn to make the bells ring, instead of waiting for the music.

The last point raises an important issue in mature relationships. During the honeymoon phase it is easy to get aroused. Sex is new and the threat of getting hurt has not yet surfaced. Many couples mistake the disappearance of this instant arousal for the disappearance of passion altogether. Nothing could be further from the truth. Arousal in mature relationships usually follows from intimacy, rather than preceding it. As I have been saying throughout this book, the best way for partners to build intimacy is to engage in a collaborative effort to make their invisible needs visible. Because sex is so pleasurable, it becomes a natural incentive for trying to meet those nonsexual needs as they are uncovered. Listening to and mirroring each other, giving shoulder rubs that recreate a feeling of being in the presence of an idealizable other, become a prelude to sex, and sex, in turn, becomes one way among many that partners meet each other's self needs.

One of the mysteries of sex is how it can bring couples so much pleasure and also be the source of so much pain. Our culture constantly portrays images that promise to solve this dilemma. If you are rich enough, thin enough, or beautiful enough, you can have all the pleasure without the pain. But in conscious relationships, the pain and struggle are part of the experience. Conscious couples must include both a sharing of the fall from sexual grace and an appreciation of the transient blessing of grace restored.

8

Money,
Housework,
and In-Laws

I got up and went in the kitchen to do the dishes. And shit I thought I probably won't bother again. But I'll get bugged and not bother to tell you and after a while everything will be awful. . . .

DIANE DI PRIMA

Most couples don't come into therapy because of their childhood pain. They come because they are struggling with issues in the present. The most common ones in addition to sex (which we discussed last chapter), are money, housework, and in-law relationships. Couples struggling with these problems may feel that looking at childhood issues is a diversion. In the present they have bills to pay. In the present there is a home to be maintained, dishes to wash, and floors to sweep. In the present they are two adults dealing with the complex web of relationships with their own families, who often intrude on their lives or draw their energy out of the relationship. These problems must be solved if the relationship is to thrive.

But sometimes even their best efforts can't solve these problems, because unconscious factors are blocking a solution. I recently had lunch with the spouse of a friend of mine. At one point she turned to me and said, "I don't care what Bill does, I'm never going to spend my time cleaning the house just to please him." Her bitterness surprised me. I thought that they had a good marriage, and they probably do, but it is clear that housework had become a power struggle for them. My friend was defending herself against being controlled and intruded upon by her husband; housework was secondary.

This is precisely the problem with so many current issues: they become symbolic issues of survival, and the defensive self takes over. To the defensive self, it doesn't matter who pays the bills or does the dishes, it matters if you can maintain your boundaries against your spouse's intrusion, it matters if you are going to suffer seemingly life-threatening neglect from him.

Fortunately, the symbolism can work in the other direction as well. Finding an equitable solution to longstanding disputes about money, housework, or in-laws can help heal childhood pain. We can learn that problems do have solutions, and that the present does not have to repeat the past. But to do that, we must accept that stubborn, angry, or irrational responses to daily issues are part

of the mix in relationships, and that solutions come from understanding these reactions, not condemning them. Because everyday struggles are so real and immediate, it is very hard for couples
to look beyond their manifest content to the symbolic level. I spend
a lot of time helping couples to decode these issues.

Conflicts about money, housework, and in-laws have one thing
in common: they are fertile grounds for parental transference. The
person who controls the money plays a parent role in a relationship; housework issues almost inevitably replicate the childhood
scenario of a parent trying to get a child to do his chores or clean
up after himself; and, no matter how old you are, you still feel like
a child when you are dealing with parents.

Because these issues lend themselves to such parent–child
feelings, couples often take on parent and child roles when they
are dealing with them. One partner scolds or bosses, the other
rebels or sullenly complies. As with other scripts in the invisible
marriage, the best way out of these stalemates is to understand the
symbolism of these problems and deal with it directly.

THE INVISIBLE ASPECTS OF MONEY PROBLEMS

Problems about money—how much there is, who controls it, and
who spends it—are among the most common problems I see in my
practice. Some couples can't even mention the subject without
getting angry with each other. Others are embarrassed to talk about
it. They feel that they should be able to resolve things without discussion, and they are afraid of seeming to be selfish or materialistic. Such couples are relieved when I tell them that almost every
couple struggles about money issues. In these days of two-career
families and prenuptial agreements, money is not a subject that
can be easily ignored.

In our society, money equals power and freedom. If you have
money, you can do the things you want. Money is thus directly
linked to issues of independence in a relationship. If you control
the money, you control at a very basic level the choices that the
couple makes. Though love relationships are not like corporate
boardrooms, money issues often degenerate into covert or overt
power struggles.

The way money brings up feelings of independence and dependence links it directly to childhood. Even under normal circumstances, children have ambivalence about their parents' power. They want to feel protected and cared for, but they fear being neglected or intruded upon. Children who had problematic childhoods will enter adult relationships with powerful tests for their partner to pass: "Will you take care of me? (and provide the security I need as well as the opportunity to buy things that make me feel excited)," and "Will I be able to be myself with you? (by having access to enough money to make my own choices)."

Traditional marriages dealt with these issues by fixing the roles of parent and child along gender lines. In terms of money, men were the parents and women were the children. But even in traditional marriages there were exceptions, such as the man who turned his paycheck over to his wife so he wouldn't drink it up or gamble it away. In that scenario the man was the perpetual little boy and the woman the responsible grownup.

Though in today's world of feminism and two-career couples much of this has broken down, residues of these feelings remain, especially on an unconscious level. Many men still feel that it is somehow their duty to manage the money, and that they have failed as men if they don't. Many women have mixed feelings about money: they may want the freedom it brings but they may also still want to be taken care of financially.

Only rarely do these issues get dealt with directly, but they are alive at the unconscious level. The role of the checkbook keeper, for instance, is full of symbolism. In addition to the obvious fact that the person who balances and carries the checkbook has more control of the money, the checkbook keeper is the independent one who is competent and provides for the welfare of a more dependent partner. "Let me have a check, I have to buy something at the department store," the child partner will ask, just like a child asking for allowance.

Money issues tap into feelings of shame. Income and money management become measures of men's masculinity. Some men feel shame if they depend on their wives financially, or if their wives make more than they do. Women often feel ashamed of their dependency, especially in the postfeminist era, or they feel ashamed at their ambition, which goes against their own gender stereotyping. When shame is evoked, both men and women are apt to respond defensively, and the everyday issues of money management never get resolved.

Money issues also bring up the yearning for expansive feelings to be positively mirrored. Having money and the freedom to spend it can make you feel like a kid in a candy store; having an overly controlling partner can squash these expansive feelings and replace them with resentment or depression. Certainly adult partners depend on each other for advice and help to regulate their spending, but all too often this dependency devolves into transference and breeds a repetitive script.

Ron and Lisa

Ron and Lisa are a good example of how childhood pain gets played out in a relationship around issues of money. Ron was an athletic young man who lived for sports, especially skiing. Lisa had admired Ron's skill and daring. Ron needed Lisa's admiration, because underneath his athletic bravado, Ron was a very insecure man who had been very injured by his parents' intrusive criticism. Lisa sensed that he needed her admiration, and at first she was glad to give it to him. But since their meeting in college their paths diverged: Lisa is on a successful career track, while Ron maintains his "ski bum" existence, working at a sporting goods store and spending as much time as possible on the slopes. Despite their professed support for each other's choices, this difference creates conflict. Lisa knew that Ron was very sensitive about these issues, and she tried not to criticize him directly, but lately she found herself picking on him for other, unrelated matters.

Lisa was actually quite astute in knowing not to criticize Ron directly. Ron had two parents who were bitterly critical of him. Nothing he did was quite up to their standards. Not only was their love conditional but it was often impossible for Ron to meet the conditions. Lisa seemed to know how much Ron had internalized his own sense of failure for not having a better job. He wanted her to look up to him the way she had when he was skiing. She did not know how to talk about her own needs for financial security with Ron without sounding like his angry, critical mother. The irony of this is that the more she buried her own concerns, the more she began to sound like his mother when she would suddenly turn on him. When she did turn on him, Ron would attack back with all his might. This became a repetitive script that protected Ron from dealing with the unconscious pain of his parents' criticism.

Lisa had been more active in managing the finances, but Ron resented Lisa's control and Lisa resented Ron for not taking more responsibility. Recently they had been trying a new arrangement, in which Ron would manage the checkbook and pay the household bills. Unfortunately this only led to a powerful conflict.

Lisa had a friend who had been to a personal growth seminar and recommended it to Lisa. Lisa saw that it had helped her friend and wanted to go also, but Ron was adamant against it. He maintained that it was far too much money. Lisa then did something she rarely did: she mentioned the discrepancy in their salaries. "I earn more than you, and I'll go if I want to." Ron responded by getting very angry, and for a minute it looked like they were going to have a bitter fight.

Their fight could not be resolved by looking at the conscious level alone. It was too involved with Lisa's childhood issues. Lisa's father was alcoholic and given to bitter attacks on his wife and children. He was an equal opportunity destroyer at times like these, but Lisa was a sensitive child and took his attacks very personally. He would especially attack her if she "got high and mighty," that is, if she threatened to make him feel ashamed with her success at school or her popularity. Lisa's mother was cowed by her husband and rather depressed, so she did not compensate for her husband's attacks and lack of positive mirroring. Being successful and marrying someone who would not be able to compete with her success were strategies to prevent a repetition of her childhood. It insured that Ron would be in no position to use money as a weapon to control or bully her. Because of this, Lisa, though she was pleased that Ron was taking more responsibility, was also afraid that in a relationship that was more equal she would lose some of her independence, and that Ron would have the power to crush her expansive feelings, just as her father had.

It was just the opposite fear for Ron. The friend from whom Lisa had heard about the seminar had recently left her husband. Unconsciously Ron was afraid that if Lisa went to it she might want to leave him too. What appeared to be a fight about money was really a fight about the twin core issues of intrusion for Lisa and abandonment for Ron. If Ron had not been unconsciously reacting to his fear of abandonment and his longing for admiration as a wise father figure, he would gladly have sponsored Lisa going to the seminar; indeed, he would probably have been willing to work extra to pay for it. And if Lisa had not been reacting to her own father transference, she would have approached Ron about the seminar in a way that included rather than alienated him.

Issues around money too often mask other, core issues and devolve into intractable power struggles. The same holds true of another common domestic issue, housework.

HOUSEWORK

Housework ranks close to the top of the list of what couples fight about. This is especially true in a time of changing sex roles. Conflict over housework used to be about whether or not each partner was living up to gender-sanctioned expectations. Men complained about the way their wives kept the house or about their cooking; women complained about whether things got fixed or the grass got mowed. Only rarely did the conflict center on which of the two was going to do a particular job. Our postfeminist era has challenged these assumptions, and one result is that more issues around housework are subject to conflict.

Though it is still not uncommon to see the men at a dinner party raptly involved in conversation while the women clear the table, at least this does not always go unchallenged. But even couples who have made a conscious effort to divide household chores equitably find housework the source of bitter and intractable conflict. This is because interactions about housework almost always have a parent–child feel to them. In addition, many people feel a direct connection between the state of the house and their own well-being: neglect of the house feels like neglect of them. So household conflicts often involve one partner who is longing to be taken care of and one partner who doesn't want to be controlled.

For many men, marital conflicts about housework replay the oedipal scenario, leading them to unconsciously resist their wives control and to resist housework as a threat to their masculinity. Between the ages of 4 and 7 boys go through a period of exaggerated masculinity and grandiosity while they switch their identification from the mother to the father and rehearse the male role. They are likely to experience their mothers' requests as challenges to both their impervious grandiosity ("You can't tell me what to do, I'm Superman") and to their effort to assert their male identity.

Since much of this is unconscious, men frequently take a passive-resistant stance, outwardly complying but then not getting to the chore. They say, "Yeah, I'll do that in a minute," but stay glued to the tube for the next hour, completely unaware that that is exactly how they behaved as children. Yet these men are not regressed or immature in other areas of their lives. I've seen competent, task-oriented corporate executives passively resist a request to vacuum the living room.

The fact that men respond like scolded boys when the issue of housework arises puts their wives in a double bind: if they say nothing and pick up after their partners, they are acting just like their partner's mother; if they complain, the men feel like they are trying to boss them the way their mothers did. And the wives are often equally oblivious to their scolding maternal tone. I asked one woman, who was a corporate lawyer, to pretend she was talking to her secretary when she asked her husband to help around the house. The husband was amazed. "I swear, she's never once asked me like that. If she could ask me with that kind of respect, I'd feel a whole lot more like doing it."

The parent–child transference in housework conflicts works the other way as well. When a husband acts like a stubborn child, his wife may act like an angry mother, but inside she will feel like an abandoned child herself. Her longings for an idealizable partner who will create a safe and orderly environment are not being met.

Housework conflicts often evolve into pursuit and avoidance scripts: the pursuing partner tries to get the other to comply with requests to do housework; the avoiding partner stubbornly resists. As with all the repetitive scripts we have been discussing, the hidden purpose of these struggles is protection from emotional pain, not resolution of the conflict about housework. The irony is that most couples I see are completely unaware of this dimension of their dispute. Many of them could have perfectly immaculate houses if they put a fraction of the energy they put into fighting into actually cleaning up. This was true for Ron and Lisa, whose conflicts about housework were as bitter as those around money.

Ron and Lisa, Continued

Lisa wanted an equal relationship, and as part of that equality she wanted Ron to do half the housework. Ron argued that he did a lot of work maintaining the yard and cars. He had a large investment in getting recognition for these endeavors. At one point he even brought a list of all his household maintenance chores to the sessions. Unfortunately, their dispute could not be resolved at a rational level, however hard they tried. Instead of merely asking for what she needed, Lisa tried to control Ron, and Ron responded by acting like a recalcitrant little boy. "Even when I do help, I never do it well enough for her," Ron complained. "If I do the dishes, she'll come by and comment on them, or even do some of them over."

They were fighting over the needs of the self, and these needs create powerful feelings of longing and fear. Lisa wanted a partner who would take care of her and sponsor her expansive feelings, but she feared being bullied and criticized. Ron wanted a partner who would mirror his achievements, but he feared being abandoned and criticized. I felt the time had come to press them to change their script. The key to resolving childhood issues in adult relationships is in evolving new strategies for getting needs met, rather than repeating the defensive ones developed in childhood. I decided to start with Ron. "It may be true that Lisa is always critical, but you complain like a hurt little boy. Whining that your mother isn't treating you fairly reinforces Lisa's image of you as an incompetent child. You must be satisfied that you've done a good job, then stick with it."

I had Ron and Lisa discuss how Ron could demonstrate his competency instead of just complaining to Lisa that she didn't recognize it. Eventually they agreed that Ron would make a chart of all the housework and divide up the jobs. He carefully included all of the work he did to maintain things and then recorded how much time the other jobs took. If this seems like a bit much, it had a vital component. Ron was dealing with the problem as a grown man, not as a little boy.

Lisa remained skeptical and occasionally critical, but their script about housework eventually did give way to greater cooperation. As the housework fight got better, the underlying childhood issues were impacted positively. Lisa learned that not all men were unreasonable like her father, and that she could let herself be taken care of, and Ron learned that not everyone was out to criticize and control him like his own mother had.

FAMILIES OF ORIGIN

Sometime after it happened I heard a story about an interaction between my wife and my mother at her bridal shower. At one point my mother had said jokingly that she was "just loaning me to her," and my wife replied, "Oh no, you're not, he's all mine now." The thought of being fought over still makes me queasy, even after all these years. But I think most of us have felt caught between our parents and our spouse at some time.

Such theorists as Murray Bowen and Carl Whitaker have speculated that the primary task of marriage is for both partners to unhook from their family of origin system and create their own family system. Partners in intimate, committed relationships must be able to say to each other, "You come first now, you're more important to me than my parents."

Many families resist letting their children go. The parents try to keep control of the children, or criticize their choices. Some draw adult children back into the family system by having continual problems or crises. Others retain financial control of the young couple. I recently saw a couple who were living in an apartment owned by the wife's father. They were having constant fights about how well the husband was or was not maintaining the property. Underneath this conflict were issues of the wife's loyalty to her father and the husband's resentment of his father-in-law's control of their life.

As hard as the transfer of loyalty may be to achieve at the outer level, it can be even harder to achieve at the psychological level. To shift loyalty from your parents to your spouse you must leave your childhood, with its remembered mixture of pleasures and pains, and transfer your needs to your present relationship. This is especially difficult if you are tied to your family with leftover business—you feel you didn't get your needs met or the recognition or just treatment you deserved. It is equally difficult if you are tied to them by the pull of security needs: you want to stay in an emotional environment that is familiar.

The conflict between past and present underlies all of the invisible marriage. It is especially powerful when the cast of characters from the past are right here, involved in the present relationship. When your parents are involved in your marriage, there is no need for transference: the triggers constantly remind you of old longings for mirroring and protection as well as of old fears of intrusion and abandonment. For example, imagine being in the middle of an intimate discussion with your spouse when you are interrupted by a phone call from one of your parents. You talk on the phone a while, and then try and resume the conversation, but the tone has subtly changed, and the moment is lost. It's not just the interruption—it's that your feelings toward your spouse have been altered by the encounter with your parent. Your childhood self has been invoked, and your experience of your spouse is now colored by its fears and longings. You may unconsciously wish that your partner would understand you better or be more nurturing, or you may notice the troubling similarities in the injurious ways both parent and spouse treat you. Perhaps the only way you are aware of this is in a slight alteration of your mood after the phone call. The confusing emotional universe that the phone call evoked is all too typical of the problems couples have interacting with their parents. One way to understand this universe is to look at the way it taxes the boundaries between your self and two of the most intimate others you will ever encounter.

Boundaries

Creating and maintaining a boundary between your marriage and your family of origin in many ways repeats the process of boundary formation that happened in childhood. As you may recall from the earlier discussion, the ability to distinguish self from other is an essential, though often difficult, task of human development. You may have learned to preserve your individual boundary at the expense of letting another in, or you may have learned to sacrifice your separateness in the interest of preserving intimacy. Now you may long for your parents to participate in the emotions that the relationship creates: to recognize your excitement and empathize with your frustrations. This participation would help you to consolidate your sense of self in the relationship by confirming the validity of your feelings. At the same time, you may fear they will interfere or offer unhelpful advice or, even worse, that they will try to sabotage the relationship.

If your boundaries were continually intruded on by your parents when you were a child, you will have difficulty preventing your parents from intruding in your marriage. Yet, ironically, when your spouse protests the intrusion of in-laws into the marriage, you are likely to find *his* input intrusive. Your defensive self may lash out at your spouse's attempt to help you set better boundaries with your parents. To your defensive self, your spouse knows nothing about how to protect you from your parents, or how to preserve the needed tie to them.

IN-LAWS

Most couples are simultaneously dealing with two sets of families. While you are dealing with your parents and reexperiencing childhood feelings, your partner is dealing with you and his in-laws. He is seeing you respond, for better or worse, in a different context, and he is experiencing your parents through his own set of parental transferences. As with other issues we are discussing in this chapter, the problem of intrusive in-laws is very real on the conscious, daily level. When one set of parents is too controlling, or even too involved in their child's marriage, it undermines the competency and autonomy of the couple. But the fabled volatility of fights around in-laws draws much of its power from the invisible marriage.

If your spouse is caught in a parental loyalty bind, you will be flooded with your own feelings of abandonment and intrusion. You are outraged that your in-laws can so easily violate the boundaries of the marriage, and that your partner is not protecting you from this intrusion. This can replicate a childhood scenario in which you needed the protection of one of your parents from the other one's intrusion but didn't get it. So at the same time you are fighting at the outer level to protect your autonomy, you may be flooded with pain and anger about your spouse's abandonment.

It is provocative just to watch your spouse interact with his or her parents. You see the origin of the traits that trouble you, and you see the defenses he has evolved to cope with his parents. Of course when your spouse transferentially experiences you as a parent, these are the very defenses he uses against you. For instance, I know a couple where the wife complained that the husband "spaced out" when she tried to tell him what she needed. On a visit to her in-laws, she saw the origin of this defense: at the breakfast table her husband became engrossed in reading the fine print on the cereal box while his mother was telling him of all her troubles. The wife reported that she had a strong desire at that moment to run away from the marriage and never come back.

As we have been saying, the invisible marriage is formed around unconscious experiences of childhood longings and pain. When your or your spouse's parents are physically present, the pathways to these experiences are wide open, and the defensive reactions are bound to be very volatile. Perhaps only sexual intimacy makes the self more vulnerable than the experience of simultaneously dealing with parents and your partner.

Ron and Elaine

The B. family consisted of Ron, a dentist, his wife Elaine and their 7-year-old daughter, Chloe. One summer they went on vacation to a beach resort with Ron's mother, Judy. Elaine had tried to instill responsibility in Chloe by having her pack her own suitcase. She had supervised, though, and told Chloe that she needed nicer clothes and more outfits. But Chloe had unpacked her suitcase in the night and replaced it with its original contents. Now Chloe was forced to wear the same clothes three days in a row. Her mother insisted she live with the "natural consequences" of her behavior, but Grandma Judy had cast several disapproving glances, and now Ron rushed to a laundromat to wash Chloe's clothes, holding the whole family up for the morning.

When he returned, Elaine was furious, accusing Ron of undermining her discipline. "You'll ruin Chloe just like you ruined Emma (Ron's daughter by a previous marriage)," she told him. They spent the rest of the day in sullen silence. Ron was caught in a loyalty bind between his mother and his wife. When he tried to resolve the problem by alleviating his mother's disapproval, Elaine took it as a betrayal and counterattacked bitterly.

When Elaine saw Ron respond to his mother's disapproving glance by rushing to the laundromat, it was as if she was looking at an x-ray of his core self. Ron had never developed adequate boundaries with his mother. He was still "wired" to respond to her needs and judgments. If he sensed that she was distressed by Chloe's dirty clothes, it was his job to eliminate the source of that stress. Ron's father was a stern, professional man, and Ron had, almost by default, grown up quite close to his mother. He had learned that the way to preserve the needed tie to his mother was to respond to her needs, even if they conflicted with his own desires.

Elaine's remark about Ron's ruining Emma was a vicious and well-aimed counterattack to the betrayal and abandonment she felt. Elaine knew all too well what it was like to depend on someone whose primary loyalty was elsewhere: her own father had continually sacrificed the family's well-being in pursuit of his career goals. The family had moved seven times before she was in high school. She felt helpless and invisible in her family. Her defensive anger was more an attempt to restore her own sense of power (If you hurt me, I have the power to hurt you) than an attempt to deal with the problem of parenting a child together. She knew just how to make Ron feel paralyzed with shame (he had abandoned Emma for a time when he left his troubled first marriage).

Flooded with the twin shames of his tie to his mother and his flight from his first marriage, Ron withdrew from the conflict, thereby reinitiating their disengaged script. As with all such scripts, theirs served merely to preserve the relationship in the face of emotional danger; it did nothing to address the underlying issues.

Fortunately, this is not where the incident ended. Ron had been doing a considerable amount of work on his relationship with his mother in therapy, and knew that this episode repeated some of his early patterns. He wanted to share this with Elaine, but he also needed to deal with her attack. Because he had consciously been dealing with his relationship with his mother, he did not fear exposure of the issue, nor was he too flooded with shame to be assertive in defending himself. So, while Judy took Chloe shopping, Ron and Elaine were able to discuss the incident.

The first thing Ron needed to say was that he had not "ruined Emma." She'd had some problems, but she was now doing fine. Because Ron was able to affirm that in a mostly nondefensive tone, the message conveyed was "Let's not let shame and anger rule our marriage." Elaine was able to respond in kind. She had some sympathy for Ron's dilemma with Judy, but she was determined to not let her mother-in-law control her parenting decisions. Meanwhile, Judy had been a good grandmother and bought Chloe some new outfits, and both parents felt less inclined to rigidly defend their positions. Things were still a bit tentative, but they were at least able to go on with their vacation.

Understanding the symbolism of in-law, money, or housework conflicts is not enough to solve them. Even if you come to an understanding on the feeling level, you still must negotiate solutions in the world. Ron and Elaine still had to find ways to stick together as parents, and not let Judy intervene. The point of understanding the invisible marriage is for partners to become allies in making necessary changes to enhance the relationship. Consciousness needs to be accompanied with commitment for change.

GUIDELINES FOR WORKING WITH DAILY-LIFE ISSUES

As we have seen, issues of money, housework, and in-laws exist in two realms simultaneously. Solving them means finding a way to resolve the feelings and parental transferences they invoke, while at the same time negotiating everyday solutions. Couples fear that talking about deeper feelings will take them in the wrong direction—away from facing inevitable hard choices and compromises these issues demand—but dealing with feelings first can be the only way to end a power struggle or find a long-lasting solution. Here are some guidelines:

1. *Avoid sounding parental.* Scolding, nagging, or ordering your partner force him simultaneously to deal with his childhood memories and the present-day relationship.
2. *Try and communicate your feelings about the issue.* "Your mother makes me feel worthless" is more effective than "If you want to see her, go and get on a plane. Nobody's stopping you."
3. *Try, as much as possible, to link those feelings to deeper self needs and core issues.* For example, "I feel abandoned when your mother dominates your attention," or "It would be easier for me to participate around the house if I didn't feel I had to do it on your agenda."
4. *Validate both of your self needs.* Compromise is not going to happen if one person feels shamed or belittled.
5. *Be forgiving.* Try to realize that a single success is more important than a dozen failures.

Understanding the symbolic nature of daily issues is an important step toward change. In the next section, "Changing the Script," we will explore ways to move beyond the power struggle and create relationships based on intimacy and healing.

III

Changing
the Script

Couples in Crisis: When the Script Breaks Down

Having your love
I was rich.
   Thinking to have lost it
     I am tortured
And cannot rest.

        WILLIAM CARLOS WILLIAMS

Up to this point we have looked at the reasons that relationships, no matter how problematic or painful, resist change. You might liken relationships that have developed defensive scripts to old LP records when the needle got stuck. In the final section of this book we look at how the needle gets unstuck. In this chapter we discuss relationships that for one reason or another have change thrust upon them, either through outside circumstances or through the action of one of the partners. In Chapter 10 we will look at the ways partners can create change. And in Chapter 11 we will discuss how to build relationships that are based on empathy and healing.

When couples are in crisis the old marital system is stretched to its limits. Will it survive in its present form, retaining the old pattern of disengagement or pursuit and avoidance, or will it break down? And if it breaks down, will the relationship survive with a new script, or will it break up?

While crises in a relationship presents the danger of breaking up, crisis also presents an opportunity to break through—to move beyond a defensive script into a meeting of real selves. In long-term relationships the real self often exists only silently, behind the curtains, directing the invisible marriage. Times of crisis can force the real self to step out from behind the curtains and speak of old and new wounds, of needs long unmet or newly surfaced. But will the real self's voice go unheard, like a cry in the wilderness? Will it be drowned in the cacophony of two emerging voices, crying out at the same time? And how can a couple, in the midst of crisis deal with the day-to-day problems in the world?

As a couples therapist, I am intimately familiar with crisis: it is the point when many couples come into treatment. They are angry and scared. They feel terribly betrayed, but they are also afraid that they will lose what security they have in the relationship. They are unable to understand how it is that they can have such contradictory feelings. They feel tremendously angry, yet they still might feel very attached to their relationship. "Is it possible that I still love my partner, when I feel this much anger?" they wonder.

These contradictory feelings often trigger rapid shifts in mood and action. During a crisis a couple's emotional life swings wildly, from packing and leaving one minute to passionately making up the next. In addition to the events that triggered a crisis, this emotionality can be scary in itself. Not only is the relationship out of control, but each partner feels internally out of control. Yet, in my experience, most couples can survive and even profit from crisis.

The task for a couple in crisis is to reestablish some emotional control without burying the feelings that are coming out. The key is a commitment to stay in the relationship and to improve communication. I emphasize commitment because times of crisis can be so painful and disorienting. When long-pent-up feelings are expressed, the picture can look very bleak. "Can it be that you've felt that way all along, and I never knew?" partners ask themselves. Of course, some of the anger is real, and some is self-protective narcissistic rage. Couples in a crisis question their own perceptions to the point where they not only feel that they can't trust their partner, but that they can't even trust themselves. The threat is twofold: they are afraid for the relationship's survival and afraid for their own emotional survival. The possibility of improving the relationship may be the farthest thing from their minds—they just want the pain to end.

But the opportunity for growth and change is real. Crises can be a time to clean out the attic—to get rid of the old habits and patterns of relating that have accumulated along the way—and make room for new ones. Moreover, a couple can emerge from a crisis feeling affirmed. "We survived that one, so we must have a strong relationship." They can come to say to each other, "We've seen the worst in each other, and we're still here."

Letting go of your usual script forces you to risk new behaviors. If your defensive strategy is to always be angry, you might have to stop being angry long enough to listen to yourself and to your partner. You might get in touch with the hurt feelings that underlie your anger, and do something to change the parts of the relationship that are hurting you. If your defensive pattern is to flee from emotional contact, you might have to turn and really face your partner as well as face your own fear of intimacy.

In this chapter we describe the roots, visible and invisible, of crises. We look at the way marriages struggle to find ways of accommodating the crisis in old patterns, and the way they struggle to evolve new ones. We look at ways of surviving the hurt feelings, of limiting the damage that is done to our trust and positive feelings. And we describe ways to use the crisis as a springboard to growth.

WHAT CAUSES SCRIPTS TO BREAK DOWN?

Tolstoy's famous statement that "each unhappy family is unhappy in its own way" applies to couples in crisis as well. Sometimes the precipitant of the crisis is obvious: an affair has been revealed, a job pits one partner's career against the other's. But many relationships reach a crisis point without the drama. They just come to a point where the status quo, the defensive script that the couple created, won't do any more, and even as a trained observer I have trouble locating the reason.

One of the tasks of a defensive script is to keep the amount of feeling in the marriage at tolerable levels. Even angry couples have a way of breaking off the fight when it gets too heated. Many couples are able to maintain their script through the most trying circumstances. I have seen couples who have a disengaged script remain disengaged through the death of a close family member, and I have seen couples who continue their anger script in any circumstance, from a funeral to one of their children's wedding. But as durable as these scripts often are, they do break down. Events can simply cause a marriage to be flooded with too much feeling for the old system to regulate.

Outside Circumstance

A death in one partner's family, a loss of a job, or a serious illness will strain a script to the breaking point. At these times the bereaved partner needs extra support, but this support requires that the other partner drop his part of the script and really be there. However, since the script was designed to buffer the perils of real intimacy, this is often difficult to achieve, despite the best of intentions. The vulnerability of the needy partner magnifies these failures. He or she may find himself screaming (either internally or out loud), "What kind of a person am I married to, who would abandon me at a time like this?"

The most difficult situations for a marriage are those that affect both partners equally. The death or serious illness of a child places an almost intolerable burden on a marital system. Infertility, which brings disappointment month after month, is another potential source of crisis. Each partner is yearning for the other's support, but both are too flooded with their own emotions to give it.

One thing that happens in the face of outside stress is that one or both of the partner's usual defenses stop working. For instance, in an anger script couple, one partner may be so upset by a turn of events that, instead of fighting, she grows silent and withdrawn. Instead of discharging her feelings by yelling, she stays with them long enough to feel sad. Instead of defensive anger, she allows her real self to feel emotional pain. This can lead to a demand for change, or it can lead to resignation. In a pursuit/avoidance couple, the pursuer may feel so dissatisfied that he just gives up the chase or seeks satisfaction outside the relationship.

The Family Life Cycle

Normal life developments can precipitate a crisis. We are all familiar with the empty nest syndrome, when couples suddenly find themselves needing to reinvent their relationship after the children leave home. In fact, all during a relationship the normal cycle of life can defeat the protection of a repetitive script and expose the couple to powerful feelings. The birth of children is an obvious example. Even the most disengaged of couples has to find some way to cooperate around parenting, while other couples must leave off arguing or pursing and avoiding each other long enough to take care of the kids.

Less obvious is the way a child's development can trigger heretofore unconscious memories or feelings of the parents' own childhood. A 2-year-old's stubborn defiance can remind a parent of her own struggles to set boundaries against an intrusive parent; a 4-year-old's heroic fantasies can remind his parents of the cherished ambitions or dreams they have given up; and an adolescent's budding sexuality can bring up the issue of sex in the parents' marriage.

Individual Growth

One of the most common factors that causes a script to stop working is the personal growth of one of the partners. Personal growth may be precipitated by any number of things: new friends, new interests, a new career, a change in family of origin. One woman had always put her own needs on hold to take care of others. In her marriage her own career and interests took a back seat to her husband's. When her very dependent mother, who had been divorced for many years, met someone who was very devoted to her and remarried, the woman reported, "I'd never thought it was possible for someone in our family to have a good relationship. I thought my mother would just go on depending on me until she died. Then I thought, if change can happen to her, why not me?" The woman began to claim time to pursue her own interests and to demand that her husband show interest in the things that she was doing. At first he resisted, and their emotionally disengaged script turned angry. But eventually they were able to reestablish a stable relationship that allowed more room for both partners to be individuals.

Personal Therapy

When one partner begins to deal with his or her deep feelings in therapy, it can change the relationship system in unpredictable ways. Sometimes there is a kind of vicarious benefit to the other, who sees his own truths reflected in those his partner is discovering about herself. Other times it is destabilizing. As the partner in therapy deals with her core issues of abandonment or intrusion with a therapist, she won't need the protection of a repetitive script in marriage as much. As the real self emerges in therapy, so do long-suppressed needs for mirroring emotional contact. This can be confusing to the other partner, who suddenly feels that the rules have changed. Some couples struggle through this confusion and learn to meet on new ground, while in others change is resisted and struggle continues. In one scenario the couple stays together but grows disengaged—the partner who is in therapy begins to seek connections for her emerging self outside of the marriage.

One potentially deleterious effect of individual therapy is that, while it helps the real self's needs to emerge, it can raise unrealistic expectations. The person in therapy begins to compare his partner unfavorably to his therapist. The other partner can come to see the therapist as a kind of romantic rival. Of course, the expectations that a spouse be as responsive as a therapist are unrealistic. Therapy, like parenting, is inherently a one-way situation. The tensions created by therapy can often be absorbed by the marriage, or even enliven it, but when it starts to seriously destabilize the marriage the couple needs help, either in the form of treatment for the other spouse or in couples treatment.

If the other person is not also in therapy, he may find that his own issues are being uncovered, but that he has nowhere to go with them. This can be very threatening, and the threatened partner will often go to great lengths to start the old fight or pursuit/avoidance script going again. This is provocative for the other partner: the spouse's lack of change can be read as a lack of caring.

AFFAIRS

Extramarital affairs threaten the survival of relationships. They create deep wounds of abandonment and betrayal, wounds that take a long time to heal, if they ever do. It is difficult for a therapist, when faced with the powerful emotions that the revelation of an affair can evoke, to keep the deeper issues of the relationship in mind. Couples in crisis feel like they are on a sinking boat. As a therapist I am often concerned with whom to rescue first, and how not to get dragged into the water myself.

But the ability to eventually deal with the underlying issues that led up to the affair may be the single most important factor that determines whether the relationship will recover. Even if the couple maintains that they never had a conflict before the affair, or even if they cannot think of a single good thing to say about each other, extramarital affairs arise out of the history and context of a relationship, and are intimately related to the invisible factors that we have been discussing in this book.

Sometimes the agenda for the person who has the affair is an end to the relationship: the affair becomes a vehicle to make this a foregone conclusion. If this is the case, the best thing a therapist can do is to bring it out in the open and facilitate the termination of the relationship. The abandoned partner may hope the therapist can work a miracle, but if the partner who has had the affair does not want to look at the issues that led to their actions there is nothing a therapist can do.

Other times it is not nearly so clear. The affair can be a desperate attempt to communicate something otherwise inexpressible. In my experience affairs can represent two very different needs in a relationship. On the one hand, they can be an unconscious cry for real change. These affairs have the unconscious purpose of creating a crisis that will shatter the protective script and allow for real feelings to be communicated ("I can't go on fighting like this," or "I can't go on being this disengaged"). On the other hand, an affair can be just the opposite: a desperate attempt to hide the underlying problems behind the affair and maintain the old relationship system.

There are a number of ways that affairs can actually become part of a couple's protective script. One is *triangulation*. Triangulation involves bringing a third party in to try to divert a conflict. Many children are triangulated into their parents' conflicts. If you were part of a triangle as a child, you might find it comfortable to create another triangle when conflicts arise in your marriage. If you were a source of comfort to one of your parents after a fight, you might look for similar solace outside your own relationship when uncomfortable feelings arise. In this way, the triangulation of an affair works as a kind of a buffer to regulate the intensity of a relationship. When threatening conflict arises, the partner who is having an affair can rush off to his lover, rather then staying with the fight and getting to the underlying issues.

Though this kind of triangulation can sometimes work in the short run, protective scripts that involve affairs are usually unstable. Even if you are not intending to destroy the relationship, such a strategy is playing with emotional fire.

Another way affairs can work to maintain a protective script is by a defensive process known as *splitting*. Splitting involves dividing the world up into rigid categories of good and bad. It is a defense that involves returning to the emotional extremes of early childhood. Sex is often the source of splitting. Because there is much shame and negativity in our culture around sexuality, it is easy to split the world into those who are sexual and hence "bad" and those who are unsexual but carry the "good" qualities of kindness and stability. The highly sexist phrase "There are some girls you marry and some you have as mistresses" is a reflection of this split.

Because sexuality can be associated with feelings of being dirty or shameful, some people divide up their intimacy. They relate to a "good" nonsexual partner, and channel their sexuality into a "bad" but irresistible lover. This protects them from having to deal with the intimacy of a relationship that is both physically and emotionally close.

JULIA AND STAN: A CRY FOR HELP

Some affairs are not so much an attempt to shore up the defenses of a relationship as a reflection that they have already broken down or outlived their usefulness.

Julia and Stan were a rare example of a couple where an affair actually led to positive change. Julia is a tall, attractive woman of 25 who came to see me feeling guilty and confused. She had begun an affair with Dan, a traveling salesman. "He's good-looking and all," she reported, "but he's not even my type. I don't even find him that interesting to talk to, but I can't stop thinking about him." Julia had broken off the affair, but it didn't end her torments or her guilt.

After a few weeks of individual therapy, Julia decided to tell Stan, her husband of three years, about the affair and to try to work on the relationship. What emerged when I saw them together was that Stan and Julia had a disengaged relationship that Julia had outgrown. Julia's parents were both alcoholics. She grew up in a swinging scene that moved from resort to resort. No one paid much attention to her needs. She was dressed in fashionable clothes, but then brought to parties and forgotten for hours. Or she would stay up half the night comforting her mother when she went on what Julia described as "one of her crying binges."

A relationship with Stan offered powerful compensation for such a childhood. Stan was a stable and caring man. Though he was about the same age, he treated Julia like a daughter, listening to her feelings, helping her fill out job applications, supporting her through one of her frequent illnesses. Beyond the protection of this father–daughter relationship, real intimacy was rare indeed. Sex had become infrequent, and most nights they stayed home watching television.

At first such a stable, disengaged relationship had been just what Julia needed. It allowed her a stable platform for her to enter the world of work and make friends of her own, something she had never had as a child. But eventually Stan's lack of emotional availability and the intrusion of his treating her like a child became too much for her. She needed more excitement and more freedom but, because she was so grateful to Stan for getting her out of her childhood environment, she did not know how to ask for these changes. So instead she ended up acting out her needs.

Stan was very hurt and stayed withdrawn for many months. He was angry and defensive when Julia tried to tell him what she needed changed. But slowly he began to see that she did want the relationship to survive, and he began to see that there were positive things for him in the changes that Julia was asking for. Like many men, Stan had learned to hide his own needs behind a mask of being a good provider and husband. Eventually Stan was willing to risk expressing more of his real feelings and asking for things from Julia that he wanted. He didn't become a true romantic, but he stopped acting like a controlling father and let himself have more fun in the relationship.

DAMAGE CONTROL

The feelings that flood a couple in crisis—shock, fear, outrage— are very difficult to control. Where the old script functioned to contain these feelings, now they feed off each other and are amplified. As the defensive script breaks down, long-buried hurts emerge that may have nothing to do with the original issue. These "laundry lists" of hurt feelings add to the mutual distress. The fact that these lists contain a mix of real and defensive anger adds to the hurt and confusion. Couples may wonder, "If there is this much history of hurt feelings, is there any hope for us?"

The first step for containing a crisis is to admit that you are in one. Often one or both partners will be in denial. Admitting things are out of control forces you to feel the feelings of hurt and desperation. If your partner is minimizing things, you will feel even more alone and desperate. The more you feel, the more you want your partner to understand the depth of your feeling and, if he fails, your defensive self will take over and try to protect you from this intolerable abandonment. However, if both partners can admit that things are in crisis, than they have at least provided some mirroring for each other. It is a first step out of their terrible aloneness.

Once you have acknowledged the problem together, you can began to try and deal with it. The following are some do's and don'ts for managing a crisis in your relationship.

1. *Don't try to bury hurt feelings.* They must come out, both to be felt by you and to be heard by your partner.
2. *There must be controls on abusive or dangerous behavior.* If you feel that things are going to get out of control, stay away. Often a cooling off period is needed. These cooling off periods must be accompanied by a commitment to discuss the problem again at a later date; otherwise they will be perceived as abandonment.
3. *Create safe forums for communication.* The presence of a friend or family member can be helpful. One good way to handle charged emotions is to set up a time-limited meeting. One person can talk for ten minutes without interruption, and then the other. After the other person has spoken, their partner should try and repeat back, as accurately as possible, and without editorial comments, what they have heard.
4. *Do talk from the point of view of your own feelings, rather than blaming your partner.* This is difficult to do in a crisis, and no one will be able to do it all the time. But "I feel very insecure that you lost your job. I'm worried about how we'll survive" is more effective than "What, you bum, not again!"

5. *Do set up "time out" periods where you don't talk about the problem.*
6. *Don't keep the problem isolated within the couple.* Do seek outside support, both as individuals and as a couple. You will find that even your friends with the most "perfect" relationships have often gone through similar crises.
7. *Do try to remember your strengths, both personally and as a couple.* Think about times in the past where you've made it through hard times. Without talking yourself out of being hurt or angry, try to also remember the things you like about your partner.

RECOVERY

As a crisis begins to settle down, a couple starts to warily try to reconnect. Something has been lost: the old sense of security and the sense that they knew each other. There is much to grieve. There may be a sense of relief that some roles have broken down. It may not be immediately clear which part is the baby and which part is the bathwater.

One difficulty is dealing with the disillusionment that has occurred, both between the partners and toward the relationship itself. During a crisis, your partner stops being a source of self needs. He may be too angry or withdrawn to mirror you, or she may have done something so outside the realm of your expectations that she no longer seems to be someone who is a kindred spirit, meeting your alter ego needs. Since crisis often brings out the worst in us, you may have trouble rekindling your admiration of your partner, and so suffer the loss of him as a source of safety and understanding. As the relationship stops being a source of sustenance, you begin to question whether you even want to continue trying to save it—you believed you had a good marriage, but now your certainties are replaced by doubts.

The disillusionment that happens during and immediately after a crisis also brings up pain from childhood. All of us have to give up our idealized picture of our parents and replace it with a more realistic one. However, if your ability to idealize one of your parents was abruptly interrupted or shattered by a childhood event, such as a divorce or a shameful revelation, you may have suffered what Heinz Kohut called a *traumatic deidealization* and you may spend a lifetime trying to replace him with a more perfect other. A crisis in your relationship can recapitulate the childhood deidealization. Then you are simultaneously dealing with two sources of pain. Your defensive reactions to this "double whammy" add fuel to the already burning relationship fire.

Even as things settle down, the residue of hurt and deidealization make it hard to reconnect. Even if your partner makes a sincere effort to provide your self needs—to listen, to anticipate and meet your needs, to participate more actively in the things you are interested in—your defensive self is liable to keep your longing for these experiences safely hidden. Instead you are liable to notice every lapse, every cue that signals a return to the old script.

Even if 90 percent of your interactions do not meet your self needs, the remaining 10 percent are the hope for the relationship. If you and your partner can consciously decide to put aside the fear and hurt and have a good conversation, or even a good time, it means something different than the good conversations or good times that happened before the crisis—it means you are consciously trying to change the script. We will discuss ways to build forgiveness and change your relationship in the next chapter.

RESISTING CHANGE

Surprisingly, one of the most common outcomes of crisis is that very little changes. One partner's stubborn refusal to change his part in the script will gradually succeed in eliciting the old responses from the other. One or both partners may secretly long for the security of the old pattern, or the sheer weight of the years of acting the script will make it feel hard to change permanently. Like a rock slipping down a hill, the old script will gather renewed power. When you think of the emotional danger that crisis plunges couples into, it is not really surprising that their defensive selves would try to recreate the old patterns in an attempt to preserve the needed tie.

Systems theorists use the term *accommodation* to describe the process whereby either an old script gets reestablished or the system changes in ways that keep the old protection in place. Of course accommodation isn't a conscious process. The defensive self moves in mysterious ways. It can lead us to make choices we don't fully understand. The wife who, several months after her husband begins to show renewed interest in the relationship, takes a job that involves travel didn't sit down and think, "Well, if I get this job I won't have to risk intimacy." But the upshot is that the old disengaged script gets recreated.

There are four common types of accommodation: role reversals, script substitutions, creating another problem, and triangulation. An example of *role reversal* is when, in a relationship organized around one partner's problem, the other spouse develops his own problem after his partner improves. One woman became agoraphobic shortly after her alcoholic husband became sober. For these couples, having a problem at the center of the relationship allows them to deal with the problem instead of risking dealing with each other.

Script substitutions involve one protective script replacing another. A couple that has been disengaged may start to fight, or a couple may fall from a pseudomutual closeness into an angry script or pursuit/avoidance. In one couple, the wife went to individual therapy and came to understand the causes of her anger. She came to see that anger kept her from feeling the threat of being abandoned. As she grew in this way, she became less vocally angry. When her husband found that he could no longer provoke her, he began to withdraw. The woman had grown to the point where the anger script didn't work for her anymore, but she was still too afraid of abandonment to risk real intimacy or consider leaving the relationship. Instead, she let her husband drift away and she herself began to be less emotionally involved in the relationship. They had merely substituted a disengaged script for their earlier one.

Sometimes couples become "crisis junkies." They live from trauma to trauma, from problem to problem. A family member is sick, a cousin needs a place to stay, there is a problem at work or a political fight in an organization they belong to. Rather than creating an opportunity for change, crises for these couples provide an opportunity to keep avoiding real intimacy. The emotions that go into the problem divert energy from the relationship itself. Requests for intimacy or focus on their own problems get diverted. One partner is likely to say, "How can you ask me that now, in the middle of such and such?" Though there is a lot of action in these couples' lives, they prove the adage "The more things change, the more they stay the same," because all of the crises enable the couple to interact in the same old way.

We introduced the concept of *triangulation* in our discussion of affairs earlier in the chapter. Children are often prime candidates for triangulation. A child will develop a problem to divert attention from a marital crisis. In one couple, the man grew tired of their pursuit/avoidance script and was seriously contemplating leaving. Just at that time, their daughter began having problems at the private college she was attending and came home for one semester. The couple was able to focus their attention on her problem, and the crisis died down. The husband was no more available and the wife was just as angry in her pursuit of him, but focusing on the daughter's problems turned the temperature down on their own crisis.

Accommodation is the way the new opportunities in a relationship get derailed back to the same old script. Now let's look at a couple, Bill and Evelyn, for whom a crisis led to permanent change.

BILL AND EVELYN

To everyone who knew them, Bill and Evelyn seemed like a happy couple. They had met after their children had grown and their careers gelled; theirs was a second marriage for each of them. Perhaps most importantly, they met in their AA program, where both, after years of sobriety, had become respected elders. Safe from the ravages of their former lives as alcoholics, they looked to all the world like a perfect couple and a model of recovery from the terrible disease of alcoholism. Unfortunately, a crisis revealed to them that, in reality, their lives were, as Bill put it, "like two trains on separate tracks," avoiding both old pain and new intimacy.

Bill was his mother's miracle child. She had almost died in childbirth and later came to invest in Bill her hopes and expectations that he would be different from his alcoholic father. As a result, he felt that he had to be perfect. He always tried to be, in his words, "a people-pleaser." Since intimacy might reveal the parts of him that were less than perfect, he tried to avoid it, first with alcohol, then, when he became sober, behind all the trappings of a successful "program" lifestyle.

Evelyn grew up in a triangle between her depressed, angry mother and her alcoholic father. Her father had life and energy, but he was always letting her down or embarrassing her. Her mother was stable but dour. Her relationship expectations were colored by these two experiences. She feared that if she let herself get close to someone she would either be embarrassed and let down, as she was by her father, or smothered in depression and anger, as she was by her mother. As a result, Evelyn learned to be fiercely independent, to avoid intimacy and keep her disappointments to herself.

Bill and Evelyn's disengaged script broke down in one "moment of truth." Though there probably were many things leading up to this event, there came a time when Bill could no longer keep looking perfect, and Evelyn could no longer keep from expressing her feelings. This event happened after they had been together for several years. They were on their first real vacation together, a trip to Europe. At the car rental counter in the airport, Bill went to check in for their rental car, but something stopped him and he asked Evelyn to handle the paperwork. It turned out that Bill did not have a valid driver's license, and had been driving without one for many years. Bill had gotten some tickets years ago, and was ashamed to go to the Motor Vehicle Department and clear them up. As a consequence he had no credit history and always paid cash. Evelyn actually knew this, but at this moment "something snapped" for her, and despite their script of conflict avoidance and denial, she became enraged and confronted him.

In a session upon their return, Evelyn described what happened to her. "I just felt that it was all a lie . . . that all of Bill's suave manners, all the respect his friends had for him, could not hide the fact that his life wasn't together. I felt like I'd been pretending all my life, pretending I was cared for and protected, when actually I was completely alone."

The incident at the car rental counter was the last straw for Evelyn. She had spent a lifetime in denial, pretending things were all right when she actually felt abandoned. And now a lifetime of feeling ashamed and abandoned came flooding into her and spilled over into the relationship. Of course, she had done a lot of work on herself to prepare for this moment—getting sober, looking at some of her own issues as an adult child of an alcoholic—but this incident was when all that work came home for her.

Instead of a partner running on parallel tracks with him, Bill suddenly found himself with a partner who was very angry and confrontive. "You don't know what your secrets do to me," she said. "I can't live like this any more. I've got to feel like you're playing with a full deck. I've got to know that you are really going to protect me." Bill tried desperately to deflect her anger. He acted contrite, promised to do more work on himself, to go to more AA meetings, but Evelyn was not appeased. She was after a real response from Bill, and would not stop until she found some reaction from him that she could believe.

It would have been easy for Evelyn to leave at this point. Once she had identified Bill with her father, she could have gone back into her "I don't really need anybody" defense. All her life she had been terrified of hurting a man's feelings, or of being hurt herself if she showed vulnerability. But this time she felt that she had too much invested in the relationship, and in her own personal growth, to settle for one more failure.

Staying in the relationship meant not only facing Bill; it meant facing her own feelings. To her unconscious mind, the car rental episode was a concrete example of her worst fears. Just when she felt trusting and expansive, she would be abandoned and embarrassed by her father's irresponsibility. "It reminds me of all the times my father would do something to embarrass me. I'd be going out with friends and he'd say something vulgar. I was even embarrassed that he was home so often in the daytime and that he didn't work like other people's fathers. I just can't live with any more surprises. I know he's not like my dad in many ways—he's stopped drinking, and he has a really good job—but I feel like I've got to set a limit somewhere."

One thing that made it possible for Bill to hear Evelyn's anger was the way she connected the events at the car rental stand to her own childhood issues. Evelyn knew that some of this was her problem. She was saying that, because of her childhood issues, she could not take this part of Bill's behavior any more. She was changing the terms: where before the goal was simply to avoid repeating childhood pain in relationships, now she wanted this relationship to be a place she could resolve it.

Nonetheless, it was terribly painful for Bill to hear Evelyn's anger. He believed that if Evelyn saw underneath his persona of the people-pleasing professional, she would stop loving him. But Evelyn wasn't abandoning him. On the contrary, she was pursuing him, not letting him disappear. Bill was in a lot of pain, but I also sensed that something else was going on. Evelyn's anger had struck something real inside of him.

"You know, I almost feel relieved. Even though the fact that I did not have a license wasn't a secret, it felt like a secret. I knew Evelyn was uptight about it, but she never said anything." A secret that was common knowledge but never commented on was ominously reminiscent of his childhood, where no one ever mentioned his dad's drinking or the terrible fights between his parents. In the absence of any comment, Bill felt that it was up to him to save the family, and the way to do that was to be perfect. Of course, that was impossible: "I could never fix it. I could never be good enough to live up to my mom's expectations, to the family's expectations. I've been running away from the feeling that I'm a failure all my life. I've never had any peace."

Bill had transferred his family dynamic to his relationship with Evelyn. He felt that he had to be perfect to be loved by her, and he felt that he had to make up for her childhood pain, just as he felt that he had to make up for his own family's pain. Not having a driver's license was a symbol of his real self saying, "I'm scared too, I don't really have it all together." At one point he turned to Evelyn and said, "I can't make it all better. I can't protect you from the fact that your dad was a drunk." In the face of Evelyn's confrontation, Bill was able to make one of his own, saying to her that he could not be responsible for her pain any more. This was his real self crying out from underneath the protection of his perfection defenses and their disengaged script.

As often happens when a script breaks down, I could see both Bill and Evelyn getting scared. Evelyn moved to try and make it all right for Bill, but I stopped her. "Your honesty is the best gift you can give Bill," I said. Bill started to be overwhelmed by feelings of shame. "There's been so many situations I've run from. Because I didn't have a license, I didn't have any credit cards. I've always carried cash, lots of cash, just like I did when I was an alcoholic and would be on the streets for days." Though this kind of chain of remembrances can be very useful when defenses break down, I felt that it was taking him out of the present moment. I directed Bill to look at Evelyn and see if he could tell what she was feeling. Evelyn replied to his inquiry, "I think that you're a beautiful person. You are kind and gentle and handsome."

"Even if I'm not perfect?"

"Especially if you stop trying to be perfect. But I do need you to get a driver's license. I'm not going to let you off the hook on that one." I suggested that it might be easier for Bill to get a license if he really felt that he did not have to be perfect. Then he would not have to be so afraid of what the person at the window would think.

This incident at the car rental stand marked a turning point in Bill and Evelyn's relationship. Though there were many opportunities to drift back apart after the feelings died down, they resisted them and instead built on the new openings for intimacy. Bill even began asking her for support for areas in his life that were troubled. He began to feel that if he didn't have to feel ashamed of his failings in front of Evelyn, maybe he didn't have to be ashamed at all. Her love and acceptance helped heal his childhood wounds. He did get a license and took steps to clear up his financial life.

The driver's license incident also made a change in Evelyn's life. Instead of running away when she felt threatened with abandonment, she was able to confront the situation and demand change. Instead of the scared little child trying to prop herself up by telling herself, "It's okay, I can handle it," she was able to be an adult saying, "It's not okay, I need better." And she found that, unlike her family of origin, her relationship could change. Bill did hear her pain, and he did get a driver's license and get his financial life in order. This enabled Evelyn to start making some other necessary changes in her life. She reorganized her business and began to take more time for herself.

Of course, no individual changes overnight, and no relationship does either. In times of stress Bill and Evelyn still tended to drift apart and fall back into their old disengagement. But the crisis was an opening, and led to a new direction that their relationship could take. Once they saw the new direction, they still had to keep making the choice to take it. Developing a conscious relationship involves constantly making the choice to risk replacing the old protective script with real intimacy. In the next chapter we will discuss ways that couples can make that choice.

10

Changing
the Script

I would be
met

and meet you
so,
in a green

airy space, not
locked in.

Denise Levertov

There is a moment in therapy when I come to believe that the couple will be able to change. It is not usually a dramatic moment, when a deep secret is revealed or a lot of feeling is expressed. It is more often a quiet moment, when one partner speaks from the center of his or her experience and the other is able to listen. Sonja and Greg had been working in therapy for about four months without much progress. One session Sonja was able to say to Greg, "I'm afraid of you when you yell. I get so jumbled inside I just turn off. You may be completely right, but I don't hear a thing." Greg started to defend himself, stopped, and was quiet for a moment.

Let's widen our focus and consider what is going on in this moment. Sonja and Greg are two people encountering each other from inside their history of a lifetime of disappointments. Sonja wishes she had a husband who wasn't so angry, who didn't make her feel so little and confused. Greg wishes his wife wouldn't distort his intention and mistake his passion for danger. Both know that their partner is far from ideal. An ideal husband would know his wife felt shattered inside when he yelled, without her having to tell him. An ideal wife would be able to mirror her husband's passion and conviction, even if she didn't agree with him. And yet, in this moment, they are able to set aside the defenses these disappointments have created and meet each other. In the next moment or the next day or the next week they may be back at their script, Greg harping, Sonja outwardly pretending to listen, inwardly retreating to a private place of refuge. But this encounter of their real selves can be a beginning. The rhythm of success and failure they experience now will be part of what they come to assimilate as the possibility of the relationship. They must not get falsely hopeful, nor crushingly disappointed. There will be no second honeymoon. But there is the possibility of change, the possibility that they can have a safer relationship, that they can have an impact on each other. In this chapter we will look at ways couples can consciously create these moments and build on them to create lasting change.

INSIGHT VERSUS ACTION

There is much discussion among couples therapists of the relative merits of insight work versus work that suggests behavioral change. I believe that change cannot come without first creating a safe environment, and that understanding both your own and your partner's own experience is the best way to create that safety.

Nonetheless, there clearly comes a point when just understanding the problem is not enough. New Yorkers have a saying that goes, "That and a token will get you on the subway." Insight will give you a map of the train system, but insight alone will not get you to your destination. There comes a time when you must turn insight into action. If you are in a disengaged script you have to stop and really talk to each other. If you are in a relationship where anger predominates, you have to stop yelling and start listening. If you spend your energy pursuing or avoiding, you have to both make a commitment to stop and face each other. If you hide your conflict under a fantasy of perfect oneness, you have to learn to communicate about the real issues and feelings you have.

Creating a healthy relationship requires commitment—not just the necessary commitment not to leave when the going gets rough, but a commitment to making your behavior more conscious. Sooner or later you must ask yourself, "Do you want a relationship that protects you from reliving childhood pain, or do you want a relationship that heals it?" Changing a relationship requires each of you as individuals to commit to changing your own behavior, as well as a mutual commitment to try as a couple to change your script.

In this chapter we will discuss four steps you can take to change your relationship:

1. Communicating your real needs.
2. Changing your part in the relationship's problems.
3. Negotiating new agreements.
4. Building forgiveness.

These steps are not meant as a formula, but only as areas where most couples need to work. Some relationships will have a harder time with one of the steps than the other. Some couples communicate well, but still have a hard time agreeing to make deep changes; other couples are able to change externally, but there remains a lot of hurt and anger; and some couples have the hardest time forgiving past hurts and moving on.

COMMUNICATING YOUR REAL NEEDS

In the example at the start of this chapter, Sonja was able to tell her husband, in a way that he could hear, what she experienced when he yelled at her. She was taking a risk, a risk of letting her true self speak without any defensive protection.

One way to understand what went right in the encounter between Sonja and Greg is to look at what could have gone wrong. Sonja could have said exactly the same message, but in a way that communicated to Greg that she was still seeing him as a bad, abusive parent. For instance, she could have sounded like a victim, complaining how unfair Greg's treatment was. And instead of hearing Sonja's experience, Greg would have heard, "You're an impossible man, just like my father was. I have no hope you'll ever change." It is a question of who is speaking, the real self or the defensive self. The real self wants its needs met; the defensive self disguises those needs to protect itself.

How was Sonja able to step out of the world of endless repetition and risk something new? I believe it was because she came to believe in the validity of her own experience. The most important thing I do in couples therapy is listen to each partner's experience. This does not put me in the middle of their disputes. Rather, it lowers each partner's sense of being unheard and defensive. Beneath this defensiveness there are feelings that long to be expressed and acknowledged. The respect I give for each partner's experience models an important mode of relating for the couple, but, more importantly, it leads each partner to respect the validity of his own needs and the reality of his own pain.

If you understand the dynamics of the invisible marriage you will have some idea of where your pain comes from, and what you most deeply want from your partner. One of the basic insights is that you may have developed a relationship that recreates some of the most painful parts of your childhood. This insight can lead to great sadness, even despair, but I think a healthier way to use this insight is to tell yourself that this relationship shows you where your individual work is. It is not enough to know that your husband is unavailable in the same way your father was. You still must learn to unhook from hurtful or destructive patterns of relating. And you still must take responsibility for asking for what you need from your partner. As with all of the steps described in this chapter, this one involves a risk. It can be terribly disappointing to invite your partner to listen to your real needs and feelings and find him stuck in his own defensive script. Yet being willing to tell your partner what you are feeling and what you want is a powerful intervention that in and of itself can change a relationship system.

What most couples need to communicate is their need for safety from abandonment, intrusion, and shaming messages. The following table will remind you which types of hurt feelings pertain more to abandonment, which to intrusion, and which to shame.

Table 10-1   Feelings Associated with Core Issues

Abandonment	Intrusion	Shame
Lonely	Controlled	Bad about yourself
Uncared for	Criticized	Always mess up
Rejected	Discounted	Your needs are wrong
Unsupported	Not trusted to do things right	Too excitable
Ignored	Guilty doing what you want	Immature
Misunderstood	Obligated	Ashamed of your appearance

These types of feelings alert the defensive self that the past is repeating itself. When you are able to identify these feelings you have to make a choice: do you want to respond to them with your defensive self, or do you want to deal with them in the present? The way to come into the present and change the script is to take responsibility for setting boundaries about the behaviors that caused you to feel this way. By saying to your partner, "When you say that sort of thing I feel ashamed of myself," you are saying to yourself, "I don't have to live in a world where shame is used to control me."

Once you have a sense of the things you most need to communicate to your spouse, it is important to do it right. Here are some guidelines:

1. *Emphasize feelings instead of accusations.* Accusations put the communication in the realm of who's right and who's wrong. These trigger a defensive reaction in your partner, and lessen the possibility of an open, understanding response. Feelings, on the other hand, are incontrovertible—no matter who's responsible, this is the way it feels. When you express your feelings rather than accuse your partner of wrongdoing, you are asking for empathy, and you are more likely to get it.

2. *Ask for change instead of placing blame.* Effective communication not only communicates feelings, it also contains a request for action or change. Learning to ask for what you want instead of blaming your partner for not giving it to you is probably the single most important thing you can do to improve your communication. Learning to change blame statements into requests puts the emphasis on change. Blame describes the way you perceive your partner, while requests for change say, "Let's make this a more satisfying situation."

3. *Be active instead of passive.* You cannot simultaneously assert yourself and play a helpless victim. Communicating what we want from our partner forces us to take an active role. And once you have conveyed your needs directly, you do not have to do so passive-aggressively by sabotaging the relationship. Often the very act of taking an active role in communicating your needs is enough to change a repetitive script.

4. *Slow down.* Much of my work with couples is getting them to slow down their reactions to each other. I sometimes use the metaphor of a slow-motion replay camera. When things begin to escalate, it's necessary to back off and slow down a bit. Sometimes a time out is useful, but it must be accompanied by a commitment to finish the conversation, or else one or both of the partners will feel abandoned.

CHANGING YOUR PART

Once you are better able to communicate what you are feeling and what you want, instead of accusing and blaming your partner, the stage is set for the most important part of breaking a repetitive script: changing your own part of the script.

It starts with me. Though relationships are a system, though you are influenced by many unconscious factors, the will to change your relationship must come from inside of you. It is far easier to point your finger and blame your partner for what's wrong with the relationship than to see your own part and resolve to change it. Your partner's faults are so evident, they have hurt or frustrated you for so long. You need so deeply to feel that you can have an impact, to know that you can get your partner to respond to your needs. You feel that if you admit the validity of your partner's criticism, all will be lost, you'll be the bad guy, and they will get off scot-free.

It takes courage and determination to take responsibility for your part in a relationship. You can almost feel the balance shift inside you when you do it. And this shift can have immediate effects on the relationship. "She's withholding, she's frigid, she's absolutely emotionally unavailable," a man is complaining, as he has been for months. "So what's your part in making that happen?" I'll ask, and suddenly he seems to get it. "I'm after her all the time. I guess I approach her with a lot of negativity." "Why would you ask her for contact in a way that you know is going to get you rejected? What's in that for you?" I'll ask, pressing the point. He'll hesitate, try to avoid the oncoming recognition, but then, "You know, I guess I have gotten used to the fight. Maybe it's safer than being close. If I get rejected, I know how to handle that. Maybe if she was really available, I'd have a hard time letting myself trust it."

When one partner owns his or her part in the relationship dynamic, it feels in the room as if a spell has been broken. Long buried, feelings of relief and softness appear on faces that moments ago were chiseled in hardness. The wife responds, "I've felt so hurt by all your blame. It's just amazing to hear you admit that you had a part in it. I've been so angry at you. Even when I felt turned on to you, I've stopped myself. I just wanted to punish you. If I saw you as all bad, I didn't have to risk opening up to you."

Taking responsibility for your part in your relationship involves two steps. The first is taking responsibility for your own behavior, and seeing how you help create the problems in the relationship. The second is realizing that you have an unconscious stake in maintaining the problem.

To start taking responsibility for your own behavior, it is useful to accept that *there is an element of truth in how your partner sees you*. Of course he distorts or exaggerates, and of course this injures you, but if you spend all your time being defensive and never take time to listen to what your partner is really saying about you, nothing is likely to change. One man kept maintaining that he was a good listener, but his wife kept saying that she felt discounted. "I hear every word you say," he insisted. And it was true he did record her statements, but only because he was formulating a rebuttal. For him to take responsibility for his own behavior he would have had to say, "You're right. I have a difficult time respecting your thoughts and feelings."

It is easy to focus on the inflammatory or indirect ways that your partner communicates and dodge what he is saying. His feelings and complaints may come out indirectly, as when he criticizes the way you are with the children, when he is really talking about the way you are with him. Or he may distort the literal truth or offer a "laundry list" of complaints that make it almost impossible for you to respond to any one in particular. All of these are "red flags" that make it easy to react rather than listen. But a first step in taking responsibility for your part in the repetitive relationships is to stop reacting to these red flags and listen to the underlying message.

One key to listening instead of reacting is to remember also that there is no one truth, and that your own point of view will not be wiped out if you listen to your partner's. If you are constantly fighting to maintain the integrity of your own experience it is very difficult to listen to another's. But if you can say to yourself, "I know I am right about the ways John is impossible," then you can also say to yourself, "Maybe there is truth in the ways he sees *me* as impossible."

The commitment to looking at yourself from your partner's point of view is a commitment to finally becoming an adult. Children see everything from their own point of view. In part this is because their selves are just developing, and their own perceptions and desires are vulnerable to intrusion by the powerful adults around them. Slowly, as their self consolidates around a sense that their own perceptions and feelings are real, children learn that there are other points of view, other feelings to consider. If this developmental process was derailed by their parents' abandonment or intrusion, it will be harder to see the other's point of view in an adult relationship. If you have trouble validating your own experience because you were required to see things from your *parent's* point of view as a price for being loved, the first and necessary step toward change must be to work on communicating your own needs and feelings.

After acknowledging your contribution to the relationship's problems, you must recognize your unconscious stake in maintaining them. Let me illustrate this with an example. A client of mine named John had a pattern of choosing women who were very independent and emotionally unavailable. This choice led to a pursuit/avoidance script. John felt angry at these women. He had been the apple of his mother's eye, and he couldn't understand why they would not give him the same kind of love his mother had given him. It took John some time to see the part he had in creating and maintaining this script, and it was even harder to see that he had an unconscious investment in keeping his partners distant. To see that, John had to challenge the myth that he really wanted a relationship just like the one he had with his mother. He had to admit the way the tie to his mother felt intrusive. In order to be the apple of his mother's eye, John had to be an apple—bright and shiny. In pursuing an unavailable woman John found a way to free himself from having to live up to her expectations, and he found a way to channel his unconscious anger at his mother into complaints about his girlfriends. His pursuit/avoidance script created a safety zone in which a push–pull battle substituted for real contact. At the same time, it kept the hope alive that, if he only pursued hard enough, he would eventually find a woman who would meet his needs.

It is not necessary to understand all of the unconscious feelings that led you to create your defensive script, but it is necessary to begin looking inside for the answers, rather than to continue blaming your partner. The key to beginning to change your scripts is the willingness to begin looking at them as protection. Just asking the question, "In what way do I benefit from my relationship script?" turns the situation on its head. Now a pattern that had been oppressive can begin to look like a puzzle that needs solving. Now a power struggle can be turned into a cooperative investigation.

STARTING SMALL

Once you have taken responsibility for your part in maintaining the relationship's script, the next step is to change it. This begins with a single action, not with a commitment to universal change. If you are a distancer, the first step is to say to your partner, "Let's have a date on Friday night." If you are always angry, it starts with a commitment one time to stop yelling and listen to what your partner is trying to say to you.

Starting small may seem futile, compared to the size of the problem, but it's not. Your defensive self created its script by matching present relationship experience with childhood pain. Even a single successful relationship experience is a step toward deconstructing the underlying belief that the past is doomed to repeat itself. Each relationship success becomes a new reality for the real self to assimilate into its sense of what is possible.

For example, a woman named Rachel came to realize that she had an unconscious investment in her husband Daniel's career problems. Daniel was an independent financial planner, and everyone agreed he was good at what he did, but he would get depressed for weeks at a time, and during that time he would let his business slide. Rachel came to realize that when Daniel was feeling better and his business was doing well, she grew testy, as if she were unconsciously waiting for him to fail. When Daniel was depressed, she could feel powerful and feel like she was providing answers. Most importantly, she was protected from having to risk relying on someone to take care of her. In fact, Rachel's fear of Daniel's success was so powerful that she actually undermined him by scrutinizing all of his business decisions and conveying the message that she was sure he was going to fail again soon.

Rachel saw that her criticism played a part in maintaining Daniel's depression. It was not the whole problem, but it was the one part she could do something about. Rachel eventually made a commitment to be less critical and to let Daniel run his business on his own. There were some setbacks, but Daniel did much better financially, his depressions lessened (and they learned to cope with them better), and Rachel was able to express her fear of dependence more directly.

These initial successes go a long way to change a script, just by creating new possibilities. But eventually couples need to negotiate conscious agreements to replace the unconscious safety their script was providing.

NEGOTIATING NEW AGREEMENTS

Just sitting down and trying to negotiate agreements in a relationship sends a message to your childlike defensive self that says, "There are adults in charge here now, you don't have to protect us any more." If you do not understand the unconscious dynamics of the invisible marriage, you would think that creating a marriage based on agreements would be relatively straightforward: I'll agree not to nag if you'll agree to do the dishes. Of course, when we look at the way the wife's nagging is organized by an unconscious belief that she must remain in a powerless position (conveyed by the hopeless quality of her tone) in order to maintain intimate contact, and the way the husband's refusal to do the dishes goes back to a struggle to wrest his newborn maleness from his mother's control, we see the task in a truer perspective. And we understand again why wresting conscious control of our behavior in relationships is often so difficult. So a single step toward negotiating a solution to a single problem can bring a powerful change to a defensive script.

BETH AND TOM

Let's take an example. Beth and Tom had an extremely angry script. Their relationship had deteriorated to the point where all they did was accuse each other and trust was almost nonexistent. It had gotten so bad that Beth was on Tom constantly about housework and responsibilities and Tom had several times spent the night at friends' houses rather than come home. They seemed to be a couple on the brink of divorce.

Tom felt that no matter what he did, Beth was going to be furious at him. His defensive self told him that she was always going to intrude on him with her irrational rage, and that he'd better fight to the death or prepare to flee for his life. Beth's defensive self told her that Tom was going to abandon her no matter what. He'd never give her the support she needed and he might leave at any time. So her defensive self told her to fight at all cost.

Beth and Tom needed to have something that worked in their relationship, something that would reestablish trust. They had company coming, and Beth wanted the spare room cleared out and painted. Tom wanted to go fishing. This dispute was one more symbolic battle over the issues of intrusion and abandonment. In therapy, I suggested that they try to reach an agreement that would take into account both of their needs. At first they reacted to this request by running their anger script of mutual accusation.

TOM

> I've tried to be reasonable, but she's never satisfied. I took down the pool table that was in the room, and I'm getting ready to paint it, but she's never satisfied.

BETH

> That was only after I asked you six times and started to do it myself.

THERAPIST

> This is more of your old script. See if you can discuss getting what you both want.

BETH

> I want the room painted this weekend.

THERAPIST

> If the room is painted, does it matter to you whether or not Tom goes fishing?

BETH

> I guess not.

TOM

> That's fine. I'll paint the room Friday night and Saturday morning, and I'll leave for the lake on Saturday afternoon.

THERAPIST

> Now, let's get this clear. Are you saying that you won't go fishing until the room is painted? And are you, Beth, saying that if

Tom paints the room it's completely all right with you that he goes fishing for the rest of the weekend?

[They both agreed.]

This seems like a fairly small step, but for Tom and Beth it was very big indeed. It was the first time in several years that they had been able to negotiate a way out of a conflict. When they reported the next week that things had gone according to the plan, they both seemed very relieved.

STEPS TO NEGOTIATION

There are some things about the way Tom and Beth's negotiation went that are important for all couples who are trying to replace defensive scripts with conscious agreements:

1. *Start small.* Even though the issues in Tom and Beth's relationship were very big, they had to start with something concrete, with a specific room that needed painting and a specific fishing trip. Global statements such as "You always . . . " and "All you ever do . . ." go nowhere.
2. *Stick to what you want.* Tom wanted to go fishing, Beth wanted the room painted. You may not get all of it, but it's best to start with a clear statement of what you want.
3. *Stay concrete.* Not "Don't worry, I'll get it done," but "I'll get it done by Saturday morning." Not "You can go fishing when you want," but "I have no objections to your going fishing from Saturday afternoon through Sunday if you get the room painted first."

Staying concrete and specific like this gives a couple the opportunity to reverse the process in which the unconscious focuses on a specific troubling detail and ignores everything else. For instance, some of Tom and Beth's most bitter fights happened when Tom was out with one particular friend of his named Bill. A few times, earlier in their relationship, Tom and Bill had come home quite late, and now, no matter what Tom actually does on a night out with Bill, Beth goes ballistic. But having had the experience of a few successful negotiations, Beth has other choices than this defensive one. When she finds herself in a pivotal moment between old, transference-based expectations and new possibilities, she can look back to this concrete experience and remember that this one time she didn't yell and scream and the room got painted. Experiences like this, in which both partners dropped their defensive scripts and still got what they needed, are like seeds of a crystal, around which a new relationship pattern can grow.

In order to establish long-lasting change, couples need to negotiate understandings and agreements about larger relationship issues. Primary among them are safety, boundaries, and intimacy.

Ultimately, couples need to decide what kinds of things are out of bounds, even in the heat of conflict, even when real and vital issues are being discussed. One wife needed her husband to agree to stop saying she was acting just like her mother. The husband came to understand that whether his observation was right or wrong, it pushed her back into an old place of defensiveness. One husband needed his wife to stop threatening divorce, even if he knew she didn't really mean it. Another wife needed to know that, when her husband stomped out of the house in anger, it was just to compose himself, not to leave forever.

Agreements around boundaries help the couple share the task of seeing that each of their selves is safe from intrusion. One husband decided that his wife needed her own voice mail to solve the way she felt intruded on when he listened to her messages. Another couple decided that the specific financial details of the husband's business would be private unless he agreed to share them. Another couple decided that, because of the wife's greater need for solitude, she could have several days a month to be left alone.

Negotiating new agreements around intimacy are especially important in changing disengaged and pursuit/avoidance scripts. If a couple can agree to get a babysitter once a month and to alternate who plans it, they have made a significant step toward undoing the defensive roles that they so easily fall into. Some couples have difficulty with the idea that intimacy must be planned and agreed upon, rather than just happen spontaneously, but that is what it takes to create opportunities for your real selves to meet.

The point of negotiating such agreements is not to create relationships that are rule-bound and inflexible, but to create a structure to fall back on. You must always keep in mind that you are fallible and that your defensive selves are very powerful. You must have space to allow yourself and your partner to make mistakes. The failure of one partner to live up to an agreement is often used by the other as an excuse to start their old defensive script. The point of reaching new agreements is that they engage the couple in a collaborative process of change.

We turn now to the last of our steps toward change: letting go of the past and forgiving.

BUILDING FORGIVENESS

We are told not to hold grudges and that to forgive is divine, but letting go of past injuries is a hard thing for most of us to do. It is made doubly hard by the fact that past emotional injuries have registered in our defensive self, which is now determined never to let us be hurt in the same way again. It is said that time is the great healer, but as we have noted, in the unconscious, there is no time, only the present moment of past events intensely reexperienced. Forgiveness means letting time proceed forward, letting the light enter the dark place where emotional injuries are stored. But how, in the face of the tremendous pull to live in past defenses, can we do this?

Consider a couple whose relationship has ground to a halt because the husband has done something very hurtful to his wife. The wife fears that if she lets go of her hurt, she is freeing her husband up to hurt her again, and the husband feels that if he lets his guard down and admits his culpability, she'll attack him and hold it against him for the rest of his life. And so, despite their underlying wish to move on, their defensive selves control the script, the incident is never mentioned, and they remain emotionally distant. In order to have a reconciliation, they must be sure that they will not be traumatized again. Here I believe the process of individual psychotherapy, which leads you to let go of injuries from childhood in order to live in the present, provides some useful insights.

One of the most important parts of the therapy process is naming and validating the injuries you experienced as a child. As you recall, this is one of the important self needs we mentioned in Chapter 2. Most of us have a sense of unreality about our childhood experiences—they happened so long ago, before we were fully conscious. We may wonder if we did something to deserve the experience. In relationships these self-doubts may also be present, in the form of such questions as "Am I being too sensitive?" or "Did I do something to deserve it?" The danger here is that forgiveness can come to mean letting go of the reality of the injury or the validity of your hurt feelings. This loss of validation would be very damaging to the self, so it is very important, in working with both childhood and relationship pain, not to confuse forgiveness with denial.

The best source of this validation is, of course, the responsible party. A spouse who can validate the truth of his partner's pain is preparing the way to forgiveness. But even if your spouse is too defensive right now to offer it, you can still seek validation from others. It is often the case that both spouses in a conflicted marriage will get validation from their friends and family. This doesn't necessarily fan the flames. In fact it can be a necessary foundation for moving toward forgiveness and reconciliation.

Distinguishing between denial and forgiveness lowers the defensive self's grip on the injury. Once this distinction is solidly in place, and you know the validity of your pain, the process of forgiveness can go forward. I believe that the single most important factor in building forgiveness is the restoration of empathy in a relationship. Part of my job as a psychotherapist is to look underneath what someone says or does and to understand *why* they do it. I find that if I let myself imagine what it is like to be the other person, I can understand the purpose of their actions, even if they have done something self-destructive or destructive to those around them.

Of course, it is much harder to be understanding when you yourself have been injured by another's behavior. When someone close to you has hurt you, it is natural to see him as a bad person who did it maliciously. To protect yourself from further injury, your defensive self is liable to lock in this sense of your partner's badness and not let any of his or her future actions change it. But if you are to let go of the hurt and forgive your partner, you must develop some empathy for what he or she did. This does not mean rationalizing it or excusing it. It just means understanding how a flawed fellow human being, acting out of an excess of defensiveness or poor impulse control, could have made a mistake. Empathy means feeling with another person. In order to do this you must be able to imagine that you felt so hurt or so threatened that you could have said or done the same kind of things your partner did that hurt you.

At some point in the forgiveness process, a kind of deal is struck. The injured spouse says to his or her partner, "I will remove the threat of retaliation, and I will lower the defensive wall I have put up between us, if you will listen nondefensively to the way your actions have made me feel." This is an agreement to have a new kind of experience, one in which the two participants do not get hurt again.

Of course the most important part of the forgiveness process is the ability of the person who has done something injurious to really listen to the pain his actions have caused his partner. In therapy I carefully structure such discussions. I usually offer the person who was hurt a time to talk for some amount of time without interruption. I encourage the injured partner to talk about his own experience, rather than make accusations, and I try to get the other partner just to listen quietly. If they do get defensive, I tell them that this is very hard, and that they'll get a turn to tell their side, but that for right now, their job is just to learn what their partner has been feeling. As an end of the process I try to get him or her just to mirror back, as best he or she can, what he or she heard. Of course this does not always go smoothly. But even if only a little bit of your experience gets through to your partner, it is the first step in rebuilding empathy.

Often the other partner is relieved to see how reparative this process of listening and mirroring can be. Consciously or unconsciously, he has come to believe that the only way to repair the injury is to let himself be punished for the rest of his life. This has led him to stonewall discussions of the injurious situation, and this in turn has communicated to the injured partner that he doesn't care at all.

In forgiving a partner who has injured you, two of the perspectives on relationships we have been discussing in this book are very helpful. From a systems point of view, we remember that nothing in a relationship happens in a vacuum. While this perspective does not excuse individual behavior, putting it in a context of a history of action and reaction does make it more understandable, and thus more available for empathy. From our understanding of childhood pain and defenses, we recognize that much of how our partner reacts to us is based on transference, and that transference can lead our partner to see us in ways that seem distorted and irrational.

Let's look now at a couple who, despite their best intentions, had not been able to forgive each other for past injuries.

AARON AND LAURA

Aaron had had an affair five years before he and Laura came to see me. When she found out about it, Laura had a retaliatory affair of her own, but, as she put it, "Mine was just a one night stand, while he was really involved with somebody." Their relationship had never really recovered. Affairs are very difficult for relationships. Sometimes they cannot recover at all. I felt that Aaron and Laura wished they could put it in the past and let go of it, but something was in their way.

Laura was very reluctant to talk about the past. "It's not what he did that I'm still mad about," she said, "it's his attitude. I think he has a real double standard. Sometimes I think his affair was no big deal to him, but that he's never forgiven me for mine." I asked her how she knows this. "He won't talk about it," she said. "To this day when I bring it up he changes the subject." She was certainly right as far as I could see. Aaron maintained it was best not to dredge up the past. But his apparent imperviousness was a defense against reliving emotional pain, and that under that defense was a well of self-torment.

I tried to get Aaron to talk about his affair, but he resisted me, too. "I don't see what's the use. I believe that if you make a mistake, you live by it. I hurt Laura, and I don't believe she'll ever trust me again." Aaron could not ask for forgiveness because he could not forgive himself. And his defensive self believed it was safer to live with the assumption that he would never be trusted again than to risk opening up and be hurt by Laura's anger or rejection. I told him I thought Laura might be more ready to forgive him than he was ready to forgive himself. He looked to Laura to confirm this and she nodded. "I never even knew you felt bad. I always thought you hated me, that you blamed me for both your affair and mine."

I did not push Aaron. I just told him to give the subject of forgiveness some thought. The subject of the affair did not come up for several weeks, and I was careful not to bring it up. I wanted Aaron's internal process to go on uninterrupted. What I did notice was that Aaron was much more forthcoming in the sessions. He talked much more freely, and both of them reported that their satisfaction level was increasing. Finally, after they reported a particularly good week, I asked Aaron how he was doing with forgiving himself. "We got married right out of college," he replied. "We were just kids, playing house. Neither of us had the slightest idea how to make a relationship work. When things got a little rough I took the easy way out." I asked him if he was ready to hear about some of Laura's pain and he agreed.

Laura was more than ready. "The thing that pisses me off more than anything is that he's used my affair to justify his all these years. I mean, you lied to me, lied to me about where you'd been for months. The only reason I slept with somebody else was to get back at you, to show you how it feels, but you were loving somebody, telling her things you should have been telling me." Laura was sobbing now, her body shaking.

Aaron, too, looked extremely distressed. His worst fears were coming true: Laura would never forgive him. And he felt his own anger at Laura's accusation that he felt justified, when in fact he didn't. I stopped Aaron from reacting and told him quietly that the truth didn't matter now, that there was an opening for him to try and repair the hurt he'd caused Laura, and that to do that he had to listen to her feelings.

Aaron was not an articulate speaker, especially when he was upset, but when I asked him to tell Laura what he was hearing, he managed to convey to her that he understood how betrayed she felt. For Laura, Aaron's message over the last five years that "We just have to put the past behind us and go on" was very threatening. She desperately needed Aaron to mirror her hurt feelings, and his refusal was like being abandoned all over again. So it was very hard for her now to take in the possibility that Aaron would be offering her something new.

This was a pivotal moment in the forgiveness process. The room was charged with new possibilities and old threats. I decided to step in and help Aaron and Laura with their confusion. I explained that the process of forgiveness started with a few little successes and a lot of false steps. I also told them that nothing could undo the past, and that the point was merely to repair the hurt enough to move on. The real repair, I told them, would come from living the next five years differently than they had led the last five.

Aaron and Laura struggled for many months. There were times when Laura, overcome with the feelings she had so long been suppressing, would bring up the affair again and again. It appeared to Aaron that she was obsessed with it, and at these times his fear that she would never forgive him seemed true. Then he would withdraw and Laura's fears that he didn't care would be triggered. But eventually they began to see even this struggle as part of their new relationship. Instead of having affairs or lapsing into years of angry silence, they would struggle with each other. It is this commitment to struggle together in the present, rather than to live in your own separate past, that is the essence of forgiveness.

Some couples have incorporated a process for clearing out old issues. They spend a certain time each month, or at the end of each year, discussing the ways they are still feeling hurt, and then they make a conscious effort to let go of them. One couple I know has their own ritual for New Years: they write their leftover anger and complaints on pieces of paper and then burn them in the fireplace.

In the last chapter we talked about ways to respond to crisis that can lead to lasting change in the relationship. In this chapter we discussed how to make a conscious choice to create change. But once we have wrested some conscious control of our relationship from unconscious defensive patterns, the question remains: "What kind of a relationship do we want to create?" It is to this question we turn in our next, and final, chapter.

11

Creating
the Ties
That Heal

For one human being to love another: that is perhaps the most difficult of all our tasks, the ultimate, the last test and proof, the work for which all other work is but preparation.

RAINER MARIA RILKE

. . . I come to you lost, wholly trusting as a man who goes into the forest unarmed. It is as though I descend slowly earthward out of the air. I rest in peace in you, when I arrive at last.

WENDELL BERRY

A valid criticism of modern psychology and psychoanalysis in particular is that it has many models for describing psychological problems, but few models for describing health. This is true for models of relationship as well. We have discussed the ways that relationships are unconsciously organized to protect us from reliving childhood pain. But how does a healthy relationship handle childhood pain?

In the 1970s and '80s the usual answer was that it doesn't. The ethos of that time was that both partners needed to have worked through their childhood pain on their own before they could have a healthy, adult relationship. Relationships that were organized around childhood needs were often labeled as *codependent*, a term borrowed from addiction theory. The implication was that all dependency was in some way an addiction!

In contrast to this view, I believe that the dichotomy between relationship and personal growth is a false one. I believe that it is only in connection with others that we find the depths of our humanity. The love of another human being is the door through which we let something outside of ourselves touch us, and it is through this door that all the world enters. To touch another, to hold his vulnerability in our hand like a wounded bird, is a test of our compassion. To let our defenses down, to allow another to touch our deepest self, is a test of our courage. I believe that love and relationships offer the opportunity for the most powerful kind of therapy, and that each partner is a potential therapist for the other. In my years of practice, I have learned that there are two essential components to therapy: safety and challenge. These are also the key components of the therapeutic aspect of relationships.

It is inevitable that relationships will be organized around the yearnings and fears that originate in childhood. A healthy relationship is one that both tolerates transference-based defensive interactions and also seeks to meet each partner's needs. This kind of relationship is characterized by two different feeling tones: compassion and tolerance for each partner's core issues, and courage and determination to move past those issues into intimacy. These two would appear to be opposites. One says, "I accept you the way you are," while the other says, "I need you to change." In a healthy relationship, though, they work in concert: the safety of an empathic connection enables the real self to risk intimacy, and this intimacy makes it easier to feel empathy for the wounded parts of each partner that resist connection.

Modern relational theories, building on the insights of Heinz Kohut, acknowledge the lifelong need for relationships, but they have not really described the ways adults can protect each other and meet each other's needs. Defensive relationships are organized by the belief that relying on the relationship will bring you pain. Either the tie will be broken (abandonment), or too high a price will be extracted to maintain the tie (intrusion), or we will be made to feel unworthy for wanting it (shame). In the invisible marriage the tie is maintained at the expense of intimacy.

But what bonds a couple in a visible, conscious relationship? I think there are three key components to a healthy relationship tie: (1) healthy relationships create safety around core issues to prevent a repeat of childhood pain; (2) healthy relationships build empathy around childhood wounds and core issues; and (3) healthy relationships try to meet, rather than frustrate, each partner's self needs.

I don't mean to say that only those relationships in which the partners are safe, have lots of empathy for each other, provide good mirroring and respect each other's boundaries can be called healthy, and that all others are pathological. I mean that these are signs of health in a relationship, and that their presence, in whatever amount, is a positive accomplishment for a couple.

With this in mind, let's look at how you can create a relationship that is built on both safety and new possibilities.

SAFETY

How do healthy relationships protect each partner from intrusion and abandonment? I believe that to have healthy relationships you must strive to respect your partner's boundaries and offer each other a strong sense of commitment.

Boundaries involve having one's basic right to autonomy respected. They regulate such necessary parts of relationship as privacy and separateness. Some people are not even aware of their right to have boundaries. This has been especially true of many women in the past. Much of the thrust of feminism has been to establish the right of secure boundaries for women, including boundaries against physical abuse, as well as boundaries that establish a woman's right to her own money and career.

On a more internal level, boundaries protect the spontaneity and authenticity of your own thoughts and feelings from being controlled by your partner. Healthy boundaries are like the semipermeable membranes of a cell wall: nutrients are allowed in, while toxins are walled out. Being open and vulnerable must always be a choice, not an obligation. The poet Rainer Maria Rilke sees the establishment of such boundaries as the key to marriage: "I hold this to be the highest task of a bond between two people: that each should stand guard over the solitude of the other." Rilke's notion of each partner "standing guard" over the other's solitude is important. It implies that in a healthy relationship, each partner takes an active part in supporting the other's boundaries. If your partner fears intrusion, then you must take an active step of saying, "I will not intrude on you."

Commitment in a healthy relationship involves more than just an agreement not to leave. It involves having one's rights to consistency, nurturance, and connection respected. Where boundaries establish the right to safety from feelings of being controlled, commitment establishes the right to safety from feeling abandoned. No commitment can make a relationship completely safe from these feelings. But a healthy level of commitment can provide protection from feeling constantly exposed to them.

Traditionally, commitments have been about such issues as financial support and sexual fidelity. On a more internal level, commitment is about having an ongoing sense of your partner's consistency and reliability. Looking at the parent–child relationship for models gives us several clues as to what an adult commitment needs to include to protect a couple from abandonment. It needs to insure that the relationship will continue over time and that there will not be too many unpredictable changes. It needs to insure that there will be an ongoing effort to maintain a feelings-based relationship tie, and that, most importantly, threats to break that tie will not be used to maintain power and control in the relationship. Each partner commits to both expressing his own inner world and listening to his partner's expression, and each partner commits to actively repairing that tie if it gets disrupted. While commitment has traditionally been more of an acknowledged need in relationships, many people do not really feel entitled to this inner sense of security.

A colleague of mine asked me recently if I thought that relationships could be too safe. I do. Commitment and boundaries act as containers for intimacy, they are not ends in themselves. The point is to make a relationship safe enough to allow the emergence of unconsciously held thoughts and feelings, not to cut them off completely. Just as the cold water emerging from the deep ocean is the source of rich nutrients for the fish that live on the surface, so the unconscious, with its storehouse of desires and fears, is the source of energy for a marriage.

As we discussed in the last chapter, creating healthy boundaries and a stronger sense of commitment requires discussion and negotiation. Once you have negotiated greater safety, the task remains to actively seek to meet your partner's needs.

MEETING EACH OTHER'S SELF NEEDS

Psychoanalysis draws its understanding of what the self needs for healthy development and stability from two sources: studies of caregivers and children, and studies of the patient–therapist relationship. In applying these models to adult relationships, an immediate problem arises. Parental and therapeutic relationships are expected to be mostly one-directional—the parent or therapist gives, the child or patient receives. So the question is, How much can you expect your partner to be like a parent or a therapist to you? Very frankly, you can expect as much as you like, you can try to get as much as you can, but you must, in order to have a mature relationship, do two things you didn't have to do as a child: you must act to contain your defensive reactions to the inevitable disappointments and you must try to reciprocate and meet your partner's self needs.

Let's take a minute to review the way the things we needed as a child remain the things we need in adult relationships. We needed, as children, to have someone we could depend on, someone who would cherish and respect our needs and aspirations. And we still need that in our adult relationships. We needed, as children, to have someone who would respect our individuality, support our own choices, and honor our need for privacy. And we still need that in our adult relationships. We needed, as children, to have someone to bind our wounds, to give us the balm of caring and understanding when we were injured. And we still need that in our adult relationships. Intimacy means moving beyond protection into a conscious, healthy dependency. The list of basic self needs described by Kohut and his followers can be our guide here.

Idealizing

Let's take an issue that is particularly problematic for many couples: the longing for an idealizable partner who understands what you need without your having to tell him. Though your yearning to have someone read your mind derives from the earliest moments of childhood, when your survival depended on a caregiver's ability to discern your needs, it does not go away in adult relationships. Take the example of your spouse buying you a gift: you want him to know just what you wanted, or better yet, to think of something you would want but hadn't thought of yourself! Of course, some people are better gift givers than others. The range of possibilities of your partner disappointing you are very real—from just giving money for you to buy something to the husband who buys his wife the new fly rod that he wanted for himself. If you have painful memories or unmet needs from childhood, such disappointments will be doubly painful.

What, in a healthy relationship, can be done when such inevitable disappointments as these arise? I recently worked with a couple for whom this question was relevant. Bonnie had a terrible childhood—her mother's depressions were interrupted by occasional periods of outright psychosis. Her husband, Joe, was a stable if somewhat stolid and unimaginative man. Bonnie wished that Joe would be romantic, that he would occasionally surprise her with flowers. Joe would agree, but never follow through. His own issues around intrusion prevented him from doing what Bonnie was asking for. Bonnie experienced Joe's failures as traumatic, and would lapse into her own withdrawn depression when they happened. One time I joked that I believed that she had Joe wrong, that she thought he was impossible, while I thought he was trainable. They both laughed and, still in a humorous mood, Bonnie explained to Joe all the steps it took to buying her flowers. The next week Bonnie described how a bouquet of flowers had been delivered to her office.

There was a quality of lightness and cooperation to their interaction. I've found that this quality is often present when couples begin to meet, rather than frustrate, their partner's basic needs. Your defensive self has a test for your partner: Are you going to repeat my childhood pain, or are you going to make up for it? Of course your partner is liable to be threatened by such a test. His answer is liable to be "no," or "maybe," or "yes . . . but." No one can really make up for another's past pain, and most people are smart enough not to even try, but this does not mean you can't meet your partner's needs in the present. Joe instinctively recoiled from Bonnie's test that he prove to her that he wasn't going to abandon her like her mother had.

You might be tempted to think that flowers were a fairly trivial way to meet someone's need for an idealizable other, but for Bonnie this was not the case. She had made the flowers a symbol for what it would be like to have an idealizable partner. Bonnie was tempted to reject the flowers because she had to work so hard to get them. But looked at another way, they were a success. As a child you pretty much have to stay with the hand you are dealt. Getting the flowers from Joe meant she could change the cards. Even though she had to coach Joe to do it, those flowers on her desk meant to her that she was in a new relationship universe, rather than living in the past.

Let's look briefly at some ways adults can meet some of the other self needs.

Mirroring

Actually, good communication meets much of this need in and of itself. When you are listening nondefensively to your partner, your posture and body language convey a sense of responsiveness. Your responses will likely be in the same tonal range and volume as your partner's. On the other hand, if you are listening defensively, you will likely respond with greater volume, or a tone that is more intense. At a nonverbal level, your partner feels "wiped out" rather than mirrored when this happens. For couples who have a hard time mirroring each other, or when the tie between a couple has been severely damaged or broken, I prescribe mirroring exercises, such as the one I described in the section on forgiveness in the last chapter. In these exercises I coach each person to carefully reflect exactly what they heard their partner say, without any editorial content. Since mirroring forms the basis of the parent–child tie, it is often necessary to begin with mirroring exercises to restore a tie that has been broken in marriage.

Twinship

Even though sameness can be deadening to a relationship and diverse interests enliven it, a sense of commonality between partners is essential. It is not necessarily a matter of politics or ethnicity, though these can be part of a twinship tie. It is more a sense of belonging, a sense of a common language between you and your partner. This is a living relationship tie; it has nothing whatsoever to do with the stultifying "oneness" of the pseudomutual script.

This self need requires active maintenance in long-term relationships. Part of a healthy commitment involves not doing something to disrupt the twinship relationship without including your partner in the process. One couple shared a strong religious commitment. On the advice of his cardiologist, the husband began exploring meditation as a way of controlling his blood pressure. To his surprise, he found that it was a source of profound spiritual growth. He began attending classes in Buddhism and going on retreats. To his wife, this was a disruption of their twinship relationship, and a major threat to their relationship. At first the husband felt that his wife's distress was an intolerable kind of intrusion. Interestingly, when he discussed the problem with his Buddhist teacher, the teacher recommended that he bring the spiritual insights back to his church and share them with the other members.

Not only was this personally meaningful, it helped repair the disrupted twinship tie with his wife.

Self-delineating

In healthy relationships, each partner takes an active role in supporting the validity of the other's thoughts and feelings. We have all seen relationships like the one in Edward Albee's *Who's Afraid of Virginia Woolf*, where the partners spend their time undermining each other. In healthy relationships, partners have learned that there can be differing feelings and points of view, and encourage, rather than obliterate, those differences. When you mirror your partner you share in his feelings; when you meet his self-delineating needs you appreciate and confirm his differences.

For example, two parents are having a problem with their child's teacher. The father feels that the best way to handle it is not to make waves: after all, the school year is almost over, and if they confront the teacher she might take it out on their child. The mother insists on having a meeting with the teacher and the principal, during which the teacher agrees to change the way she handles the issue. Afterward, the father says appreciatively, "You were like a mother tiger, protecting her cub in there. I can never do that, I always want to avoid a conflict." Ideally, the wife would find some occasion later to acknowledge the utility of her husband's belief in avoiding conflict, or even of the reasons for its existence, such as saying, "Well, nobody ever fought for you in your family, so you never learned how necessary it was."

Naming and Repairing Injuries

Healthy relationships need to develop ways to get back on track when conflicts and injuries derail them. The place to start is to acknowledge your partner's feelings and experiences. Too often one partner seeks to win by discounting the other. Of course, this only escalates the problem. Now the other person is desperately trying to defend the integrity of his own experience, as well as feeling the initial injury. Naming the injury supplies a self-delineating experience for your partner in times of conflict. It is an important way of maintaining the relationship tie at these times; of saying to your partner, "Even though there are hurt feelings, I'm not going to try to destroy you."

For instance, a wife gets jealous of her husband for talking to a female colleague at his office party. The husband, feeling his own injury about her intrusion, might say, "You're paranoid, we were only talking about a project we're working on." Or he could name her experience and say, "I'm sorry you felt that way. There was nothing going on, but it must be hard for you to be here without knowing anybody."

Naming and repairing emotional injury are really two separate steps, though just naming your partner's feelings goes a long way to repairing the injury. Repair involves taking some responsibility for your hurtful actions, and offering some reassurance that your partner will be safe from a repetition of the problem. For instance, in the example above, the husband might add, "You know, I do get wrapped up in my work and forget you sometimes. The next time we go to a social event with my coworkers, I'll check in with you from time to time and see how you're doing."

GUIDELINES FOR MEETING YOUR PARTNER'S SELF NEEDS

The following guidelines summarize ways you can commit to meeting your partner's self needs:

1. Once I have identified my partner's core issues, I will actively try to protect him from pain in those areas, including respecting his boundaries and not using a threat to cut the emotional tie as a way of maintaining power.
2. I will actively try and listen to my partner, not just to the content, but also to the feelings he is expressing.
3. I will act independently, without waiting for requests, to anticipate and meet my partner's needs.
4. I will not make changes to my lifestyle, career, or philosophy so abruptly as to disrupt my partner's sense of fellowship.
5. I will acknowledge and respect my partner's thoughts and feelings, even when they differ from mine.

6. When my actions hurt my partner, I will acknowledge his pain
    and try and repair the injury.

Of course, this list corresponds to creating safety, as well as meeting your partner's mirroring, idealizing, twinship, self-delineating,
and naming and repairing injuries self needs. *Do not hold this list
up as an ideal and blame yourself for not living up to it.* No one could
live up to these guidelines all or even most of the time. Rather they
are things to work toward; any progress on them can be enormously
healing to a relationship.

THE FEAR OF GIVING

Even once you understand the nature of your partner's deepest
needs, you still may experience a strong resistance to meeting
them. This does not mean you are a bad or selfish person. Resistance to meeting your partner's needs originates in fears that seem
very real to most of us. One fear is the "stray dog theory": you fear
that if you meet your partner's self needs he will regress and grow
infinitely dependent on you. Feed him once and you will have to
take care of him forever. A closely allied belief is that there can be
only one dependent person per relationship: if you meet your
partner's needs, you will be perpetually locked into that role, and
your turn will never come. I call this belief, in which you and your
partner are rivals for scarce resources, the sibling rivalry theory.
A third reason that you fear giving to your partner is that you have
lost your ability to distinguish among coercion, manipulation, and
voluntary giving. You have been resisting so long you don't know
how to stop. Let's look at each of these, with an eye on ways to
overcome them.

Fear of Regression

This fear exists not just in relationships, but also in psychoanalysis and in our society in general. The underlying belief, which is
supported by Freud's theories, is that people develop and grow not
from having their needs met, but from having them frustrated. Such

fears permeate our society, leading to critiques of government programs to help people as well as so called "whole child" education theories that attempt to teach by meeting the child's basic needs. And, of course, at a practical level, these fears appear to have validity. If you always tie your child's shoes, it makes it less likely that he will want to learn to tie them himself.

The confusion stems from misunderstanding what needs you are trying to meet. Are you addressing the needs of your partner's defensive self or his real self? I am certainly not advocating buying a drink for an alcoholic partner in the name of "mirroring" his thirst! And confrontation can be very empathic: saying to your partner, "Don't eat that rich desert, remember what the doctor said" provides an idealizing self need that is vital.

How then are you to know when you are responding to a real need or feeding the defensive self? In the abstract, you can't. In therapy it is a process of trial and error: some of the things you do help the patient grow; others, no matter how theoretically sound, seem to keep him stuck. It is the same in marriage. But too often we fear that providing self needs for our partner in ways that seem "parental," such as anticipating her needs before she asks or taking the time to really listen to her feelings, will keep her from ever taking the initiative. In fact, coming to feel that your relationship is a place where your deepest needs can be met is highly energizing. Knowing that you have a secure and fulfilling marriage can make your life and career seem like an adventure.

Competition

A belief in scarcity runs deep. It may start in childhood, when there wasn't enough love for every child. I have seen many couples caught up in a sibling-like rivalry: they both want attention from the other, but neither is willing to give it. Each feels that if they give in and meet the other's needs, they will never get a chance to get their own met.

In one relationship the man steadfastly refused to make a commitment. He wasn't interested in other women, and in most ways he was a good partner, but he wouldn't commit to anything, even to a date a week from Saturday. It turned out that he believed that, if he gave in to meeting his girlfriend's need for security, all was lost. His deepest longing was that a woman would let him maintain his own interests. He believed that this was nearly impossible, that no one would respect his boundaries. Withholding from his partner seemed to be the only way he could keep some sense of control over his own boundaries. Of course, this was irrational—withholding all commitment drove his partner crazy, and made her more demanding—but it was very hard for him to wrest his fear of commitment away from his unconscious long enough to try to see if he could get more of his needs met by giving rather than withholding.

Giving Versus Giving In

Because your partner feels that getting his self needs met is a survival issue, he is likely to have tried everything possible to get you to meet them, including trying to bully or manipulate you. You probably developed an equally strong desire to resist this intrusion at all costs. Like the person who withholds sex because he feels obligated, even if he is turned on, you may even refrain from meeting your partner's needs when you want to.

Moving outside of this bind requires a kind of existential leap. You need to define yourself as the author of your giving actions. One way to think of this is that you are also being coerced by your partner if you respond to her demands by invariably withholding. Free action means you have a choice, to give or not to give. It is easier to say "yes" one time if you know you have a right to say "no" the next time.

BEYOND BEAN COUNTING

One of the pitfalls that couples fall into when they begin to meet each other's self needs is keeping score. Walking around with a secret tally of what you are owed will inevitably lead to resentment. If you feel that you are giving more than you are getting, try to communicate in a way that invites your partner to give more, rather than accuse him of being stingy. Of course, this bean counting is a way of protecting yourself from being exploited—it is usually organized by your defensive self.

On the other hand, when you are meeting your partner's self needs, you are really nurturing yourself as well. Just as defensive behavior gets magnified in a relationship system, cueing a return to a repetitive script, so giving can be magnified. The synergy created when you mirror your partner redounds in unpredictable and sometimes wonderful ways. One wife had been highly critical of her husband's career. It had been a thorny issue for them for many years. When, instead of criticizing him, she was able to listen to his own fear and despair about the poor choices he had made in the past, things began to change for them as a couple. It turned out that it was not really his career that worried her, it was his depression about it. The husband's confiding in his wife brought them closer, and as their intimacy increased the issues around money lessened, despite the fact that nothing changed in the husband's work life.

BUILDING THE EMPATHIC TIE

Once you and your partner have established a relationship that is safe enough to allow your defensive self to let go of your old script, and once you have established a pattern of meeting, rather than frustrating, each other's self needs, there remains the greatest challenge in relationships: to love and accept your partner where he or she is most wounded.

Emotional pain flourishes and persists in isolation, like a wound that is infected and closed over. Intimacy overcomes that isolation, and opens up your wounds to the healing light of day.

In describing the challenges of this kind of intimacy, I invoke the images of the Wendell Berry poem I used as an epigraph to this chapter: "... *I come to you lost, wholly trusting as a man who goes/into the forest unarmed. It is as though I descend/slowly earthward out of the air. I rest in peace/in you, when I arrive at last.*" Going into the forest unarmed, floating out of air into the lover's arms: images of vulnerability. We started this book with the knowledge that love is blind. To create a conscious relationship, you must go forward, in that darkness, exploring your self and the self of your beloved, by touch, by Braille. Intimacy comes into our language from the Latin for "innermost." To love another is to go into the depths. It is a reciprocal journey. You cannot go into another's depth without going into your own. You cannot love and forgive your partner without loving and forgiving yourself. And this is the greatest challenge of loving: to move beyond shame and fear into self-acceptance and self-love, and to feel that you have the power to help your beloved move beyond his or her own shame and fear.

We have talked about the hope of finding in marriage something that was lacking in your own childhood. And we have talked about the fear of actually getting it. In truth, what glitters is gold, only it is a type of gold you cannot spend until you have unhooked from your unconscious, defense-based relationship.

When I spoke earlier of partners being each other's therapists, I didn't mean that your job was to take away your partner's pain or make up for the unhappiness he or she suffered as a child. I have seen something like that happen on rare occasions, and it always seems to me to be a stroke of grace or luck when it occurs. I know a woman who suffered a truly horrendous childhood, filled with abuse and alcoholism. She is married to a very kind and steady man, and I believe that just having him in her life has been enormously healing to her.

More often, though, we find a mate with approximately the same level of childhood wounding, and try to muddle through with each other. What then is the kind of "therapy" I am speaking of? I think, at their deepest level, relationships allow you to be empathetically connected to your partner's pain, and that this witness, this acceptance, is the healing.

Empathy does not mean unqualified acceptance and participation in another's experience; that is merger. Rather it means a willingness to temporarily suspend your own thoughts and feelings and imagine your way into your partner's experience.

Self psychologists have coined the term *empathic introspection* to describe the way a therapist listens to his patient. In this model, the way into another's experience is to go deeply into your own. If you have the feeling that you can imagine what another's experience is like, it is probably because, by looking deeply into yourself, you have found analogous thoughts and feelings.

So the empathic connection is formed not only by deeply listening to your partner, but also by deeply going into your own experiences. This is why the experience of empathy is so closely connected to the experience of having a secure tie to another person: it opens a connection between your real self and your partner's.

The most profound source of empathy is the understanding that, underneath our varied defensive strategies, human needs are universal. We all want to maintain our boundaries and autonomy, we all want to maintain a tie to another. We all want to know that our deepest feelings can be responded to, and we all want to feel safe and understood in another's presence.

The way past an impasse in relationship is to develop empathy for your partner's experience. Though we're certainly not all alike, we all want the same things, in whatever different proportions. If you are a pursuer, I think you can, through introspection, find a part of yourself that wants to feel secure from another's intrusion, and that you can use this understanding to feel empathetically connected to your partner's needs for autonomy. Of course, this does not preclude simultaneously feeling your own pain and frustration about the strategies your partner uses to preserve that autonomy.

EMPATHY AND SHAME

Most of us feel that our wounding has made us defective. As we discussed in Chapter 2, this feeling of shame leads us to hide our real needs and show our partner only our defenses. Underneath even the most belligerent person's behavior is a belief that he is not entitled to have his true self mirrored, that his thoughts and feelings are defective, and that only through anger will any of his real feelings ever be acknowledged.

Of course, the first thing we are likely to do when someone hurts or threatens us is to withdraw our empathy. We feel that our partner is being willfully cruel and inhuman. But this only reinforces our partner's shame.

Empathy is the antidote to this cycle. It takes courage to open up to your partner's humanity, but it is the only way he or she is ever going to hear your requests for change. No one has ever showed his true self in response to a message that goes, "Why don't you open up and talk to me, you defective slob."

On the other hand, empathy heals shame. If your experience can be understood, than you are a part of humanity, not a shameful outcast. This is why self-help groups such as AA are so healing. I know a young couple whose marriage almost floundered because of the husband's shameful secret—he liked to rent and watch pornographic videos. Because of his belief that his sexuality was defective, he had completely closed down sexually to his wife. When he was able to tell his wife about his rigid, Midwestern Protestant upbringing, and the way the videos allowed him to preserve his sexual feelings, he was amazed that she didn't condemn him. She even offered to watch the videos with him, if he thought it would improve their sex life.

Let's turn now to an example of one couple establishing an empathic tie around very painful childhood experience.

DANIEL AND RACHEL

We met Daniel and Rachel briefly in the last chapter. Rachel was the woman who realized that her way of trying to control Daniel's business decisions was contributing to his depression. Their protective script had Rachel telling Daniel what to do and Daniel passively resisting. Here I want to describe what happened after they were able to let go of that script. Rachel was able to offer Daniel something much more profound and healing than mere protection: empathy about his almost unbearable childhood pain.

Daniel and Rachel both had childhoods dominated by their parents' alcoholism. Since it was Daniel's mother and Rachel's father who were the alcoholics, their marriage evoked a lot of transference. Each feared the other's abandonment, and they both attempted to deal with these fears by desperately trying to control the other. Rachel was constantly afraid that he would leave the family in financial ruin, just as her father had. Daniel's attempts to control Rachel were subtler. He attempted to control her emotions. He was afraid when she got too expansive or excited: it reminded him of his mother when she was intoxicated. So he would withhold sexually and would undercut Rachel's enthusiasm in other areas as well. Of course, like most such invisible marriage strategies, these only succeeded in creating a situation that frustrated them both equally.

After a while, they were able to negotiate some conscious agreements that met, rather than frustrated, their needs. Even though Rachel had no problems with alcohol, Daniel asked Rachel to agree to stop drinking for a while. He was able to get her to see that any alcohol-induced personality changes, no matter how subtle or inconsequential, filled him with intolerable memories of his childhood. Rachel got Daniel to agree to hire someone to run the financial side of his business. These agreements were important in and of themselves, but they were even more important in that they were a first step out of their invisible marriage into a conscious relationship.

As often happens, letting go of their protective script brought them hope, but it also made them more vulnerable. In the course of a few dramatic weeks, Daniel and Rachel had a crisis, but were able to move through it to a moment of profound healing. The depth of their work, of their vulnerability and their courage, was very moving to me.

For the first few weeks after their agreements, things were calm. Freed from day-to-day planning, Daniel was able to focus on the creative aspects of his business, the things that he was really good at. In therapy, I learned more about their childhoods, including the fact that Daniel's father committed suicide when he was 13. Neither Daniel nor Rachel showed much emotion as he mentioned this—it seemed like something they had already dealt with—but the very next week they were in the midst of a crisis.

Rachel came into my office trailing Daniel by several feet. She looked worn out. Her face showed that she had been crying. Before I could even say "Hello," she looked at me and announced, "It's over, David. I want a divorce." I looked at Daniel. He looked downcast. "I guess it's best. I'll never really be what Rachel wants me to be." Rachel proceeded to tell about an incident that was, for her, the last straw. They had planned a long weekend away. Rachel had arranged babysitting. It was to be a kind of second honeymoon. Just as they were about to leave, Rachel found that Daniel had forgotten to make the reservations, despite his promise to do so. "I realized I just can't go on like this anymore," she told me.

After listening to this discussion a while, I formulated two possibilities, and I decided to put them both out to Rachel. "Either your saying you want a divorce means that you have really had it with Daniel's depression, and that you are no longer willing to put up with the abandonment, or that you are so afraid that Daniel cannot deal with the pain of his childhood that you are offering him the ultimate protection: saying, 'I will leave this marriage so you don't have to deal with your pain.'"

Rachel was much less angry when she came in the next week. "I've thought about what you said, and I think you are offering us a new direction, but I don't really understand it. What does it mean to stop protecting Daniel?" Before I said anything, Daniel stepped in.

"It means my facing up to my rotten childhood. I'm just not sure that would do any good. And I'm not sure where to go. Should I see you alone, go to an Adult Child of Alcoholics group?"

"What's wrong with right here?" I replied.

"In front of Rachel? I'm not sure I could manage that."

"Why not?"

"Well, I guess I'm afraid I'd be too much for her, that she'd get upset and try to fix me or make it all better."

"But I'm here to stop her if she tries that. Is that the only reason? Look at her now and see if you can find any other reason."

Daniel looked at Rachel for several minutes. Her eyes were soft and compassionate. But something in her posture also said that she was staying separate. Daniel sat looking at her for some time. Then he began to cry, first very softly, then almost uncontrollably.

"I've tried so long to hide all this. I feel so ashamed. I want people to think I'm happy, not serious. I've always played the clown.

"I was 13. I came in and found my father unconscious. I saw an empty bottle of pills nearby. My mother was still screaming at him, accusing him of shamming it for attention. I dialed for an ambulance myself. The ambulance came and took him off. No one said anything about it. They packed me off back to my prep school. After about five days, the headmaster called me in. 'I'm sorry to tell you this,' he said, 'but your father has died.' No one was there for me. I just went back to my mates and pretended everything was okay. I guess I've been pretending ever since."

Daniel had unconsciously started looking at me while he told this story. Rachel had put her hand on his shoulder. Her look was very soft now, full of caring. I said, "Look at Rachel now and tell me what you feel." Daniel started to make a joke, but then stopped himself. He was quiet for a few seconds. "I feel loved. I feel really loved."

In that moment Rachel saw beneath the flamboyant, out-of-control, Daniel, below the depressed Daniel, below the controlling Daniel. She saw the unspoken pain he had been carrying his whole adult life. This moment would probably not solve a single one of their many conflicts and problems. But the tone of their struggles with those problems would be changed by it. They had created a bridge of empathy between two isolated worlds of pain.

I watched Daniel and Rachel walk out of my office down the hall. I knew they had a lot of work ahead of them. But there was something in their walk that spoke not of work but of lightness, of grace. As with all things that are worth doing, love is hard work. But the work is not an end in itself. Like an Olympic diver slicing into the water without a splash, the culmination of the work of love is a moment of effortless beauty and joy.

Bibliography

Atwood, G., and Stolorow, R. (1984). *Structures of Subjectivity.* Hillsdale, NJ: Analytic Press.

Bach, G., and Wyden, P. (1968). *The Intimate Enemy.* New York: Avon.

Basch, M. (1988). *Understanding Psychotherapy.* New York: Basic Books.

Beebe, B., and Lachmann, F. (1992). The contribution of mother–infant mutual influence to the origin of self and object representations. *Psychoanalytic Psychologist* 5:305–337.

Bowen, M. (1978). *Family Therapy in Clinical Practice.* New York: Jason Aronson.

Bowlby, J. (1969). *Attachment.* New York: Basic Books.

Brandchaft, B. (1994). To free the spirit from its cell. In *The Intersubjective Perspective*, ed. R. Stolorow, G. Atwood, and B. Brandchaft, pp. 57–62. Northvale, NJ: Jason Aronson.

Brandchaft, B., and Stolorow, R. (1990). Varieties of therapeutic alliance. *Annual of Psychoanalysis* 18:99–114.

Dicks, H. V. (1967). *Marital Tensions.* New York: Basic Books.

Framo, J. L., ed. (1972). *Family Interaction: A Dialogue Between Family Researchers and Family Therapists.* New York: Springer.

Jackson, D., and Weakland, J. (1968). Conjoint family therapy: some considerations of theory, technique and results. In *Therapy Communication and Change*, ed. D. Jackson, pp. 185–271. Palo Alto, CA: Science and Behavior Books.

Kaufman, G. (1980). *Shame.* Rochester, VT: Schenkman Books.

Kohut, H. (1971). *The Analysis of the Self.* New York: International Universities Press.

—— (1977). *The Restoration of the Self.* New York: International Universities Press.

—— (1984). *How Does Analysis Cure?* Chicago: University of Chicago Press.

—— (1985). Thoughts on narcissism and narcissistic rage. In *Self Psychology and the Humanities*, ed. C. Stozier, pp. 124–161. New York: Norton.

Kübler-Ross, E. (1969). *On Death and Dying.* New York: Macmillan.

Lansky, M. (1981). Major psychopathology and family therapy. In *Family Therapy and Major Psychopathology*, ed. M. Lansky, pp. 3–18. New York: Grune & Stratton.

Levertov, D. (1983). *Poems 1960–67.* New York: New Directions.

Livingston, M. S. (1995). A self psychologist in couples land. *Family Process* 34(4): 427–439.

—— (1997). *Conflict and aggression in couples therapy: a self psychological vantage point.* Delivered at the 20th Annual Conference on the Psychology of the Self, Chicago, IL, Nov. 14.

Minuchin, S., and Fishman, H. (1981). *Structural Family Therapy.* Cambridge, MA: Harvard University Press.

Morrison, A. (1989). *Shame.* Hillsdale, NJ: Analytic Press.

Napier, A., and Whitaker, C. (1978). *The Family Crucible.* New York: Bantam.

Rilke, R. M. (1984). *Letters to a Young Poet*, tr. S. Mitchell. New York: Random House.

Ringstrom, P. (1994). An intersubjective approach to conjoint therapy. In *A Decade of Progress*, ed. A. Goldberg, pp. 159–182. Hillsdale, NJ: Analytic Press.

Rubin, L. (1983). *Intimate Strangers.* New York: Harper & Row.

Scharff, D., and Scharff, J. (1987). *Object Relations Family Therapy.* Northvale, NJ: Jason Aronson.

—— (1991). *Object Relations Couple Therapy.* Northvale, NJ: Jason Aronson.

Schwartzman, G. (1984). Narcissistic transferences: implications for the treatment of couples. *Dynamic Psychotherapy* 2: 5–14.

Shaddock, D. (1997). An intersubjective approach to conjoint family therapy. In *Conversations in Self Psychology, Progress in Self Psychology, Vol. 13*, ed. A. Goldberg, pp. 289–306. Hillsdale, NJ: Analytic Press.

Shane, M., Shane, E., and Gales, M. (1997). *Intimate Attachments*. New York: Guilford.

Siegel, J. (1992). *Repairing Intimacy*. Northvale, NJ: Jason Aronson.

Slipp, S. (1984). *Object Relations: A Dynamic Bridge Between Individual and Family Treatment*. Northvale, NJ: Jason Aronson.

——— (1988). *Object Relations Family Therapy*. Northvale, NJ: Jason Aronson.

Solomon, M. (1989). *Narcissism and Intimacy*. New York: Norton.

Solomon, M., and Siegel, J. (1997). *Countertransference in Couples Therapy*. New York: Norton.

Sperlin, H. (1977). *Psychoanalysis and Family Therapy*. New York: Jason Aronson.

Stern, D. (1985). *The Interpersonal World of the Infant*. New York: Basic Books.

Stolorow, R. (1994). The intersubjective context of intrapsychic experience. In *The Intersubjective Perspective*, ed. R. Stolorow, G. Atwood, and B. Brandchaft, pp. 3–14. Northvale, NJ: Jason Aronson.

Stolorow, R., and Atwood, G. (1992). *Contexts of Being*. Hillsdale, NJ: Analytic Press.

Stolorow, R., Brandchaft, B., and Atwood, G. (1987). *Psychoanalytic Treatment*. Hillsdale, NJ: Analytic Press.

Trop, J. (1994). Conjoint therapy: an intersubjective approach. In *A Decade of Progress*, ed. A. Goldberg, pp. 147–158. Hillsdale, NJ: Analytic Press.

Weinstein, D. (1991). Exhibitionism in group psychotherapy. In *The Evolution of Self Psychology*, ed. A. Goldberg, pp. 219–234. Hillsdale, NJ: Analytic Press.

Wile, D. (1988). *Couples Therapy*. New York: Wiley.

Winnicott, D. (1965). Ego distortions in terms of true and false self. In *The Maturational Processes and the Facilitating Environment*. New York: International Universities Press.

——— (1986). The concept of a healthy individual. In *Home is Where We Start From*. New York: Norton.

Suggested Readings

Goldbart, S., and Wallin, D. (1994). *Mapping the Terrain of the Heart*. Reading, MA: Addison Wesley. An excellent book on the psychodynamics of love.

Hendrix, H. (1990). *Getting the Love You Want*. New York: Perennial Library. Very readable and full of information on parental transferences and healthy communication.

Karen, R. (1992). Shame. *Atlantic* 269(2): 40–70. A readable and thoughtful article.

Kaufman, G. (1985). *Shame*. Rochester, VT: Schenkman. An excellent overview of shame theory.

Rubin, L. (1983). *Intimate Strangers*. New York: Harper & Row. Profiles a number of couples and describes their struggles for intimacy.

Scarf, M. (1987). *Intimate Partners*. New York: Ballantine. Excellent description of patterns of couple relationships throughout the life cycle.

Solomon, M. (1994). *Lean On Me*. New York: Simon & Schuster. An excellent book for couples that promotes healthy dependency and uses self-psychology concepts.

Wile, D. (1988). *After the Honeymoon*. New York: Wiley. An excellent book on conflict and communication for couples.

Index